I0186514

DARE TO SUCCEED

Finding Passion to Fuel a Purpose-Driven Lifestyle

For Teenagers and Their Parents

by

Richard A. Sherrod Sr.

Dedication

I dedicate this book to my children, who are all successful. They have never been to jail, used drugs, or gotten into trouble. One is an architect, another a computer science expert, and another a wonderful mother. They all make me proud and remind me that all teenagers and young adults can achieve greatness. Warren Buffet said he was no smarter than the average person and that everyone could do what he did. Knowledge, preparation, and hard work are the keys to success. Teenagers need folks with experience to care for them and help them by sharing their knowledge. I learned a lot from each of my children, which reminds me that everyone has God-given talents.

I could not write this book without the support and encouragement of my wife of 40+ years. There were plenty of times I acted like a butthead, and she loved me anyway. We started a nonprofit corporation partly because she loves helping people and refused to let me simply retire. She is a wonderful Christian and role model for healthy living.

Join Our Village and Grow Your Knowledge!

Thank you for being a believer in self-help and helping others reach success. The old saying "it takes a village to raise a child" is still true today. I encourage you to sign up for updates on our website, Tips4Living.org. That way, we will update you on new podcasts, YouTube channels, e-books, and workshops to improve your life. You can get tips and ideas to enhance your life and continue to help your children live a healthy and joyful life. This "village" support will ensure we have the information needed to gain financial independence and achieve our goals.

We will start a podcast, Dare2Succeed, to discuss all the topics in this book. Experts from various fields will share their views on developing children for success. Once launched, you can find us on Spotify.

Some may need more support in completing this book's list of actions. To that end, we will launch the Dare2Succeed Learning Lab to support your efforts. The Learning Lab has three key objectives. The first enables a detailed understanding of each chapter by providing on-demand videos. The second provides learning understanding and clarification by assigning each participant a certified life coach. The third ensures all actions are completed by having each participant and life coach meet via video call as needed for support. Enrolling in the Learning Lab is free, and you only pay for each class you take. Contact advisor@dare2succeed.org with questions.

CONTENTS

Introduction

"You know you are on the road to success if you would do your job, and not be paid for it."

Oprah
Winfrey

The pace of change and innovations in technology are causing stress and depression for many teenagers and their parents. Because of this, teenagers and parents find it challenging to succeed in the 21st century and believe the old rules and methods for success no longer work. This book will outline specific ways to achieve goals that provide joy and peace. In this context, telling young people to "grind it out" is not helpful or practical. Instead, the goal is to help them find a way to love what they make money doing—after all, the pursuit of happiness is still a worthy endeavor. Success needs a process that will guide you through to completion, just like any process used at work to achieve an outcome. View this book as a roadmap for achieving success in a new way.

This book is for teenagers, young adults, and parents alike. Young people must learn how to succeed early in life, and parents must know how to coach and develop success. Since parents do not receive a training manual on being a great parent, we all learn by trial and error. While high school prepares teenagers for some aspects of success, it often falls short in teaching the real-world business skills necessary to achieve greatness. In addition, we may not realize that others have found the answers to many of life's questions. Unfortunately, many adults do not share these valuable tips from one generation to the next.

This book teaches specific ways to achieve success before graduating high school. It provides examples, solutions, methods, planning tools, models, checklists, forms, templates, and resources.

So, you may be wondering why it's important for children to start thinking about success early in life. The reason is that humans develop their interactive skills at home at an early age. Their confidence is created, in part, by the encouragement and support they receive from their parents.

I went back to college at 57 years old to get a college degree because there were specific things I needed to learn. After all, the world was changing quickly in the 21st century, and after retiring in 2018 from a large company as a vice president, I knew I wanted to start a nonprofit corporation to help teenagers and young adults succeed. The Sherrod Foundation Inc. was founded on the principle that those with knowledge must share their experience for the benefit of those coming up behind them. I completed my certified life coach training to coach people on implementing the recommendations and help them create their personalized implementation plans.

I write this book as an extension of my responsibility to share decades of learning, experience, and expertise. Throughout these pages, I know you will get ideas that encourage you to "dare to succeed" in a world that rewrites the rules for success every few years. In today's rapidly changing landscape, technology is eliminating whole industries, and skills are shifting fast.

As shown in Figure 1 below, we created a unique success model to help visualize life's critical stages and the elements you must deal with.

Figure 1

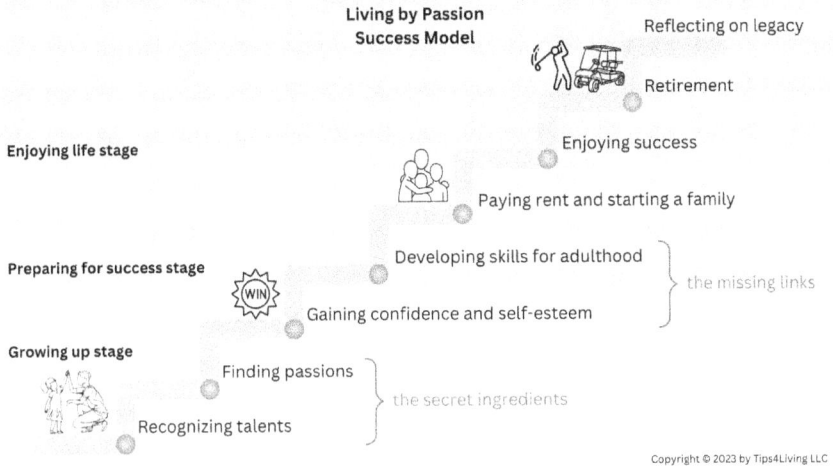

Living by Passion Success Model

Reflecting on legacy

Retirement

Enjoying life stage

Enjoying success

Paying rent and starting a family

Developing skills for adulthood

the missing links

Preparing for success stage

Gaining confidence and self-esteem

Growing up stage

Finding passions

the secret ingredients

Recognizing talents

Copyright © 2023 by Tips4Living LLC

This model includes three significant stages of life.

Growing up Stage – This is where we recognize our talents, find our passions, and gain confidence and self-esteem. In this stage, we also develop our values and habits. These are the secret ingredients.

Preparing for Life Stage – This is where we sharpen our skills for high school, college, work, and family. Growing into adulthood means getting serious about the future. We know we must put food on the table and pay the rent.

Enjoying Success Stage – This is where we enjoy life, reap the rewards from our careers, take incredible vacations, raise our families, start businesses, and retire successfully. We think about our legacy and how people will remember us when we are gone.

This book will cover all stages and elements of our model for success. We look at it from a teenage and young adult perspective, along with the role of parents and how they can help. We believe children and parents must have a common understanding of what it takes to succeed so they can have more meaningful conversations and engagements. Parents sometimes struggle to figure out how to help their children, so this book was designed to help with some essential elements. This book's structure is different from most "self-help" books. You may think this is a classroom book, and that is intentional. The idea is to cover the problem, highlight the solutions, provide the homework (actions), and complete the forms after each chapter. That way, you always know what you learned and what actions you will take.

Keep in mind that success is part of happiness. Although living your passion will bring you joy, achieving happiness is beyond the scope of this book because happiness includes complex topics like relationships, mental health, and spiritual self. Nevertheless, we will cover how to think differently about balancing work and life in Part 3. We call this approach the Four Cornerstones of Life. As you think about your legacy, we also cover the type of relationships you want in Part 5. These parts of the book help develop priorities for how you spend your time.

So, do not let this book sit on the table, and do not make excuses about being too busy to finish it. It has been said, "You can tell what's important to someone by how they spend their time."

We will cover the contents of this book in six categories:

- Part 1 focuses on recognizing your talents. We will explain how to identify your talents and isolate your passions, as well as give you ways to showcase your skills and passions.
- Part 2 focuses on preparing for success. We will teach you how to assess your likes and dislikes and turn that into a joy-filled career. The focus is on skills that support your passion.
- Part 3 focuses on developing a purpose-driven life. That means living on your terms, pursuing a purpose, and maintaining balance in life.

- Part 4 is about changing the game with your relationship with money. The rate of depression proves happiness does not come from the "hustle society." The wealth gap proves we are going about this all wrong because you can be wealthy and not be happy or at peace. We will discuss how to own your destiny regarding financial independence and peace.
- Part 5 explains planning for, implementing, and living your legacy before retirement. I guarantee you will learn several methods to showcase your legacy before you live your life. If you think this claim is too bold, flip to the back of this book and check out the legacy checklist. I know your parents or grandparents have never used some of those tips.
- The last category, Part 6, deals with the lies we see and hear on TV and social media. If you pursue a life as you see it online, it will guarantee your failure. It also assures your depression because no one can live up to the fake lives we see online. I use this part of the book as a reality check.

I promise you will get inspired and receive at least 20 things you can implement to be more successful. My ideas will not cost you much money, and you can implement most of them quickly. There is a saying, "The sooner you get started, the sooner you will finish." So, commit to reading this book within three months and recommend it to three people so they can also get great ideas. Take out your yellow highlighter to mark important points for future reference. You will want to return to many topics later, so take plenty of notes.

After reading this book, you will be able to accomplish the following;
- ✓ Complete the form to recognize your talents and identify ways to practice those talents. Identify at least two passions that give you joy and create ways to enjoy what you love.
- ✓ Complete an assessment of your skills, know what skills you love and hate using, and then complete your development.

✓ Map critical skills necessary to support your passion. Then, identify jobs and companies willing to pay you for those skills. Link your skills to your development plan.

✓ Identify who your mentors and advisors will be and document the role each will play in your development.

✓ Document your goals and understand the type of life you want to live that gives your life purpose.

✓ Learn how to build a great credit score, build generational wealth, invest for retirement, start your own business, and end the cycle of poverty.

✓ Develop, live, and share your legacy. This legacy document will ensure people know who you want to be and how you want to live. It helps people understand how you lived as they reflect on the years.

✓ Young adults will be able to have more engaging and thoughtful conversations with their parents. Parents will be able to coach and support the development of their children, which will build confidence and self-esteem.

✓ Remember that someone living their passion and getting paid for it will likely never be depressed.

Part 1

Recognize Your Talents and Passions

PART 1 | Recognize Your Talents and Passions

"The person born with a talent they are meant to use will find their greatest happiness in using it."

Johann Wolfgang von Goethe

Tiger Woods was exposed to golf at a young age by his father. He demonstrated a natural talent for golf and began playing competitively at eight. Known for his intense focus and dedication, Tiger would practice for hours, often hitting balls until it was too dark to see. He won his first junior world championship at the age of nine. Tiger's journey from a child loving golf to one of the greatest golfers of all time is a testament to his hard work, dedication, and natural talent. His story exemplifies how everyone is born with natural talents; they simply need to find their passion and work hard for it.

In Part 1 of this book, we will explore the importance of finding one's talents and practicing them to improve. We will cover why it is critical to identify those talents that make you smile just by thinking about them, helping you understand your passions and how they lead to a purpose in life. Finally, we will wrap up Part 1 with the role of parents and the dangers of social media on self-esteem and confidence.

One of the most essential steps to achieving success in life is recognizing your talents. God-given talents are the things that come naturally to you and bring you joy and fulfillment. When you understand your talents, you can develop them into skills that you can use to pursue your passions, achieve your goals, and make a positive impact on the world. These talents can also help you earn a living to pay the bills. Every person has unique talents, strengths, and abilities that can be leveraged to accomplish their goals. However, many teenagers fail to recognize their talents and often underestimate their potential. Remember, everyone has talents and natural abilities, and determining yours early in life will help you succeed with ease. With the support of parents and mentors, you can uncover your unique gifts and talents.

The first step toward recognizing your talents is identifying what makes you happy. To do so, remember those things you are naturally good at doing, and take time to reflect on your academic, athletic, artistic, or other areas where you excel or struggle. You can also take assessments or talk to your teachers, parents, or friends to get feedback on your abilities. We will cover ways to assess your skills in Part 2, which will help you identify your strengths and weaknesses.

Once you have identified your strengths, nurturing and developing them is crucial. For instance, if you have a flair for writing, take advantage of writing competitions or join the school newspaper. Similarly, if you are interested in technology, learn computer coding or artificial intelligence (AI). Many nonprofits will teach you these STEM-related talents at no cost. By honing your abilities, you can gain confidence and a sense of purpose, motivating you to work harder toward your goals.

It is also crucial to recognize that everyone has weaknesses, and seeking help or support to overcome them is okay. For example, if you struggle with math, seek extra help from a teacher or a tutor. Do not let your weaknesses keep you from pursuing your passions and achieving your goals because personal training will maximize your efforts.

Finally, maintaining a positive attitude and growth mindset is essential. Believe in yourself and your abilities, and do not fear taking risks or trying new things. Remember that success is not only about getting good grades, winning awards, or being popular but also about learning from failures and setbacks. We will take the following chapters and provide specific details on identifying and nourishing your talents and passions.

In Part 1, we will cover the following topics:

- ✓ Recognize your talents
- ✓ Showcase your talents
- ✓ Identify and enjoy your passions
- ✓ Parents, passion, confidence, and self-esteem
- ✓ Beware of social media

Chapter 1 – Recognize Your Talents

"Your talent is God's gift to you. What you do with it is your gift back to God."

Leo Buscaglia

In this chapter, we will look at how to determine and improve your talents. We have all heard of examples of child prodigies who demonstrate extraordinary abilities before the age of 10. For example, Stevie Wonder lived up to his name. Even though he had been blind since he was a few days old, he learned to write music and play the piano, harmonica, and drums while he was very young. Stevie Wonder began his recording career at age 12.

Wolfgang Amadeus Mozart composed music at five and composed symphonies before he was nine. Pablo Picasso was a great visual artist. Anne-Marie Imafidon, a Black woman, is a computing and language prodigy. She was the youngest to be awarded a master's degree in mathematics and computer science by the University of Oxford. Sierra Leone native Kelvin Doe taught himself engineering at age 13. He built batteries, amplifiers, transmitters, and other items from scrap metal and trash. He even started his own radio station. Sor Juana Inés de la Cruz learned Latin and wrote poetry at 13. By the time she was 11, Maria Agnesi could speak Latin, German, Greek, Hebrew, Spanish, Italian, and French.

Enrico Fermi demonstrated a photographic memory and spent his youth constructing electric motors. Bobby Fischer learned chess from his sister when he was six. By age 12, he was competing against America's best chess players. Two years later, he won the US Open Chess Championship and became a grandmaster at age 15. Priyanshi Somani began mental calculation at six years old, and five years later, she was the youngest participant in the Mental Calculation World Cup and won that event. Alma Deutscher started playing the piano at two and the violin at three. At age seven, she composed a short opera.

I list many examples of child prodigies to show that extraordinary talents are not rare. The list could have a thousand examples, but consider the countless talented kids who did not get a chance at fame and recognition. Children could have natural talents waiting for parents to nurture and develop.

Question: What are your natural talents? What are you good at, and do you like it?

Now, let us cover important suggestions for recognizing your talents and wrap up by highlighting how parents can help.

Everyone Has Talents—Find Yours!

The first step in finding your talents is exploring your interests. One of the most significant challenges for middle and high school students is discovering their talents. However, finding your talents is essential to achieving success in life. Do not be afraid to try new things or step out of your comfort zone—join clubs or organizations, attend workshops, or participate in community events that align with your interests. These activities can provide valuable opportunities to discover your hidden talents and passions.

While you explore these interests, don't be afraid to fail. Many billionaires have said that failure is the prerequisite to success, which means that to succeed, you must first learn from your attempts and why you've failed. This way, you know what works and what does not.

Let's look at some tips for recognizing your talents. As you read, jot down the ones that stand out. You should capture your talents now because you will need them later when thinking about your passions.

Pay attention to what you enjoy doing. Consider the activities you find yourself naturally drawn to that bring you joy—these may include drawing, writing, playing sports, or taking things apart. Pay attention to these activities and consider how to develop them further.

Another way to find your talents is by reflecting on your experiences. Think about the tasks or projects you have completed successfully in the past. What skills did you use to accomplish them? Did you enjoy the process? What did you learn from them? These questions can help you identify your natural strengths and abilities.

You should try new things and not be afraid to try many new activities and hobbies. You never know what you may discover about yourself because trying new things can help you uncover hidden talents and passions. And remember, if you dislike something or fail at it, that's part of the learning process. Living your passion also means knowing what you hate doing.

Consider your strengths by thinking about what you are naturally good at. These may be things like leadership, problem-solving, creativity, or communication. Also, consider how you can use these strengths to pursue your goals. Accepting that everyone has weaknesses is crucial, so don't focus on being perfect or let your shortcomings keep you from pursuing your passions and achieving your goals. We will cover ways to assess your skills in Part 2, which will help you identify your passions.

Many online assessments can help you discover your talents and strengths. For instance, Gallup.com has a StrengthsFinder assessment that identifies your top five strengths based on your responses to a series of questions. Similarly, the Myers-Briggs Type Indicator (MBTI) assessment by mbtionline.com helps you understand your personality type, including your strengths and weaknesses. These assessments can provide valuable insights into your natural abilities and help you make informed decisions about your academic and career paths.

It is essential to maintain a positive attitude and learning mindset. Believe in yourself and your abilities, and do not fear taking risks or trying new things. Remember that success is not only about achieving goals but also about learning from failures and setbacks. Confidence and self-esteem play a role in a positive attitude, so we will cover that in Chapter 4.

Seeking feedback from others can also be an effective way to find your talents. Ask your teachers, coaches, mentors, friends, or parents for feedback on your abilities. What do they think you are good at? What areas do they think you could improve? This feedback can help you identify your strengths and weaknesses and guide you in developing your talents further.

Keep in mind that some friends may not help you succeed. If some friends consistently give you negative input, it may be time for new friends. We will cover the impact of friends more in Chapter 13. Also, don't even think about getting input from social media due to the risk of bullying.

A Parent's Role

Parents can play a crucial role in helping their children recognize their talents. Let's explore ways parents can help their children and be their leading life coaches.

Encourage your children to try new activities and hobbies. Provide opportunities for them to try lots of things, attend workshops, or join clubs or organizations that align with their interests and passions. You either have lived through this experience or have watched others participate in these things and grow. Remember that your children do not know what they do not know, so be active in the discussion and help them generate ideas.

Provide resources and support for your child's interests. For instance, if your child is interested in music, give them an instrument or pay for music lessons. If they are interested in science, buy them a kit or take them to science museums. Many nonprofits offer these resources for free, so do your research.

Listen to your child's ideas and interests and provide feedback on their abilities. Encourage them to reflect on their experiences and provide guidance on further improving or developing their talents. If you are giving them feedback on something they are weak at, do so in an encouraging way and recommend they take a training class to improve that ability. Everyone can grow and get better, so do not focus on the weaknesses. Instead, think about the possibilities.

Be positive and supportive of your child's efforts to find their talents. Do not pressure them to pursue a particular talent or activity. Instead, provide them with encouragement and support, and let them explore and discover their interests at their own pace. Some parents may force a child into doing what the parents like because they think it is necessary for success. Parents need to remember that a child can succeed in many different ways, so don't steer them into your "old school" way of doing things. The world is changing fast, so skills and methods must change.

Celebrate your children's achievements and successes. This support can build their confidence and motivation to pursue their goals. I have seen far too many parents focus on what a child is doing wrong instead of what they are doing well, so remember that giving positive feedback will always boost a child's engagement in an activity versus constant criticism. Bake a cake and invite extended family to celebrate an achievement because children will remember those moments.

Help your child develop a "success team" of mentors and coaches. We will cover this in more detail in Part 2 for you to know who to include and why. Mentors will ensure your child gets input, feedback, and training from people who know what they are doing with the child's interest at heart. Your extended family has professionals and experts in business, finance, the arts, and training, so use them but pick them carefully.

Key Takeaways

Remember that no one can reach their destiny without cultivating their talents. Finding your talents as a preteen or teenager is a crucial step toward achieving success later in life. You can identify your natural abilities and passions by exploring your interests, reflecting on your experiences, taking assessments, and seeking feedback. The skills needed for success in the future will change, and you must continually learn new things to keep up with the world. Parents can also play a vital role in supporting their children's efforts to find their talents by encouraging exploration, providing resources, listening, providing feedback, and being positive and supportive. Finding your talents is a lifelong journey, and discovering new skills and passions is never too late.

In the next chapter, we will focus on practicing and showcasing your talents. Robin Sharma once said, "Why hide your talent in the closet of complacency when you have greatness within you?" Many teenagers and young adults have talents that few people know about, and that reality deprives the world of significant contributions. It should be noted that finding your talents is the first step. Now, you need to know how to improve them so others can see your value in what you offer. Additionally, most passions come from your list of talents, so practicing and showcasing the talents you love is a precursor to happiness.

Your Next Steps

Think about and capture your talents on the form at the end of this book. Next, write down how you can practice or showcase those talents. Engage a parent or teacher in completing this task.

Chapter 2 – Showcase Your Talents

"Talent is like a little seed—when nurtured, it will flourish."

Matshona
Dhliwayo

In the last chapter, we covered the importance of finding your talents. Everyone has talents, and we encourage you to try different things to find yours. We gave you several things to try and included ways parents can support their children in this endeavor. Now that you know what your natural talents are, this chapter will focus on the importance of showcasing your gifts. Showcasing your talents is a fantastic way to build confidence, gain recognition, and explore new opportunities. Talent needs practice to get better.

I firmly believe that perfection, as a concept, is a flaw. No one can ever be perfect. The best people can hope for is to improve and be better than anyone else. The future has a strange way of making perfect things obsolete over time—for example, young athletes improve their technique, create a unique way to win, and continue shattering records. Therefore, you should focus on the concept that "practice makes progress." In this chapter, we will explore many ways for children between 10 and 18 years old to showcase their talents and get better. We will highlight how parents can help them explore their strengths and build confidence and self-esteem.

Question: What events have you participated in to showcase your talents? What new things can you do to show others you have talents?

The Role of Competition

Not long ago, there was a practice of recognizing every child who showed up at an event and declaring them winners for participating. The problem with this approach is that you will not push yourself very hard if there are no winners and losers. We understand the impact losing has on children and how that might cause them to give up; however, the only way to get good at something is to practice. Tiger Woods once spoke about the thrill of participating in major golf events and made the point that playing against the best in the world was the only way he got better. Winning against the best reinforces the demanding work he puts into his practices.

Participating in competitions and shows is one of the most popular ways to showcase your talents and forces you to get better. Parents should ensure their child gets training for a talent or skill before encouraging them to compete. In Chapter 10, we cover the personal improvement action plan and how to complete it.

 Look for competitions or shows that align with your talents and interests, such as music competitions, art exhibitions, science fairs, or talent shows. Participating in these events can help you gain recognition, receive feedback, and connect with like-minded individuals.

Show off Your Stuff

Creating a portfolio or video is another terrific way to showcase your talents. If you have artistic skills, develop a portfolio of your best artwork. If you are a musician or performer, create a video of your best performances. These portfolios or videos can be shared with potential employers, clients, or colleges.

You can practice by helping others. Volunteering and giving back to your community are excellent ways to make a positive impact and also showcase your talents. Look for volunteer opportunities that align with your interests and talents, such as teaching music to children, editing videos, helping with a science fair, or designing a website for a nonprofit organization. Volunteering can help you gain practical experience, build your portfolio, and make valuable connections.

There is another side to helping others, where you make money by sharing what you know. Millions of people make money by doing what they are good at. If you are good at fixing things, neighbors will pay you to fix minor issues. For example, setting up a new iPhone or programming a smart TV is something most grownups prefer not to do, and they will pay a teenager for help.

Building a social media presence can also be an effective way to showcase your talents. Create a social media account on Instagram, TikTok, or YouTube, and share your talent with the world. Post videos or tutorials showcasing your skills and interact with your followers to build a community. Building a social media presence can help you gain recognition, connect with like-minded individuals, and attract potential clients or employers. Millions of people make a lot of money on social media by simply showing others how to do something. However, be aware that there are several disadvantages to being on social media, which we will cover in Chapter 5.

The Role of Parents

Parents can play a significant role in helping their children showcase their talents. The following are some ways parents can support their children in this process.

Provide resources and support for your child's talent. For instance, if your child is an artist, provide them with art supplies, enroll them in art classes, or set up an art studio in a spare room. If they are a musician, provide them with an instrument or pay for music lessons. If you do not have the money for these things, contact a local nonprofit or church—

many organizations support the success of children. You could even ask family members to give specific items for birthdays and Christmas gifts. Sometimes, children receive gifts they do not want or lose interest in others within weeks. No matter how you do it, providing resources and support can help your child develop their talents further and build confidence.

Help your child identify opportunities. Plan a brainstorming session with your child to get at what excites them. Most preteens are not excited when parents push them into sports, so expand the conversation to other things. If you know what they watch on social media, you will know what they spend time on. These things will likely make them smile, and you will cherish seeing a smile on their face.

Also, think ahead beyond the current year. The world changes quickly, and skills become outdated within a few years. If you are interested, we have an e-book that covers the economic cycles over the past 2,000 years in great detail. We do cover this at a summary level in Chapter 14 because understanding how the world changes will be crucial in helping your children succeed. For example, the Information Age was about creating, disseminating, and profiting from information. People knew how to make money. Some received college degrees in computer science, while others learned data analytics. Each of these jobs pays a great salary for companies looking for those skills. However, the next wave of change is the Automation Age. This change risks data analysis and computer programming jobs because AI will efficiently complete those tasks for a company at little cost.

Help your child narrow down the list of opportunities to showcase their talents. Look for competitions, shows, or volunteer opportunities that align with your child's interests and talents. Encourage your child to participate in these events and support them throughout the process. Many parents forget about the Boys & Girls Club or the YMCA, both of which tailor programs for exploration and building confidence. In addition, Atlanta, Georgia, has Junior Achievement, and this organization is a world standard for showcasing talent because it pairs students with a business executive as a mentor. If you're not in Atlanta, other cities have groups like Junior Achievement that focus on students' success. We will spend more time on mentors and advisors in Chapter 7.

Next, part of your role is to share your child's work with your friends, family, and community. Post their artwork on social media (do not show children's faces), share their music with your friends, or invite them to perform at family gatherings—just make sure you get their permission first. Respect is a big deal to teenagers, so remember, it goes in both directions. Sharing your child's work can help them gain recognition and build their confidence. Some parents showcase their young adult's skills on LinkedIn, a business and employment platform, to expose them to hiring managers.

Be positive and supportive of your child's efforts to showcase their talents. Encourage them to pursue their interests and provide them with constructive feedback. Remember that showcasing talents is not just about winning but also about growing from the experience. Also, remember that children take feedback more personally than adults do; science shows they may not have learned the difference between constructive feedback and criticism. Always view your feedback from the child's perspective, and your message will land better on them.

Key Takeaways

In this chapter, we covered the importance of showcasing your talents, which is an essential step toward achieving success and building confidence. Even if you fail early on, you will learn from the experience and improve. We provided tips like participating in competitions and shows, creating videos, volunteering, giving back, and building a social media presence. By implementing some of these tips, you can benefit by gaining recognition, receiving feedback, and exploring new opportunities. We discussed the importance of competition and how getting better can fuel a passion.

We introduced the concept that perfection is a flaw and that you should instead focus on progress by practicing. Additionally, parents can also play a crucial role in supporting their children's efforts to showcase their talents. We provided some examples of organizations that can help.

In the next chapter, we will focus on finding your passions. Rachel Roy once said, "Design the life you want to live." Many teenagers want to do what they love until their parents remind them of the need to make real money and pay their bills. Many teenagers and young adults have talents for which people will pay good money, but most high school graduates cannot imagine this reality because they may not have developed their skills. Far too many students do not know what shirt or blouse they will wear the next day, let alone what career they want. It would help if you focused on getting the skills you need in high school so you can hit the ground running as an adult entering the workplace.

Parents must understand that the world has changed, and Americans are consumers of "help me." That is why we spend so much time showing you how to identify your passions from your list of talents so you can help others, make a living, and enjoy what you do.

Your Next Steps

Use your highlighter throughout this chapter to mark examples you want to think more about. Then, write down how you will practice or showcase your talents. Be sure to involve your parents, teacher, or mentor in completing this task.

Chapter 3 – Identify and Enjoy Your Passions

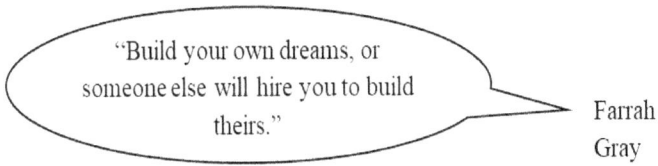

"Build your own dreams, or someone else will hire you to build theirs."

Farrah Gray

In the last chapter, we covered the importance of practicing and showcasing your talents. We discussed how competition can force us to practice so our talents improve. We pointed out that showcasing your talents can also make you money. The next chapter on passion is the longest and most important. In this chapter, we shift your focus away from success with money and focus more on happiness. As indicated in our introduction to the book, any scientific discussion of happiness is beyond the scope of this book because it includes many complicated elements. In the introduction, we introduced you to a Living by Passion Success Model created by our company, Tips4Living LLC. This chapter will focus on the Growing up Stage, where talents, passions, confidence, and self-esteem are the primary outcomes.

Before we go on, let me clarify the definition of passion. Passion is when you love what you do. Passion can be defined as a strong fondness, enthusiasm, or desire for an activity. It is an intense feeling that can motivate you to act. Passion manifests itself as a deep sense of satisfaction and joy that comes from engaging in an activity for its own sake. It is not just about liking what you do but about feeling connected to it, being motivated by it, and finding extraordinary meaning in it. Now that you understand passion better, let us dig a little deeper.

Question: What talent makes you smile just thinking about it? What excites you so much that you can't wait to get out of bed to do it?

Avoid Getting Stuck in Life

As a teenager, you need to know your passions because they help you develop a sense of purpose and direction in life. When you clearly understand what you are passionate about, you are more likely to be motivated, engaged, and fulfilled in your pursuits. Passion can drive you to work hard and persevere through challenges, leading to tremendous success and happiness.

Knowing your passions can also help you make informed decisions about your future. It can guide you in choosing your academic and career paths and making decisions about the activities and hobbies you pursue. Additionally, when you are passionate about something, you are more likely to seek opportunities to learn and grow in that area, which can help you develop valuable skills and knowledge.

Ultimately, knowing your passions can help you lead a more fulfilling life. It can help you build self-confidence, resilience, and a keen sense of identity, all of which are important for your personal and social development. Many people are stuck in jobs they hate because they do not use skills they love, and the work gives them no sense of purpose. This can lead to anxiety, stress, anger, and depression.

How to Separate Passions from Your Talent List

As a teenager, you may have various skills and talents that you enjoy, but it can be difficult to determine which ones are genuinely your passions. Some talents we use because we have to, while we use others because we enjoy them.

Over the past few decades, two events caused adults to reexamine their lives, give up using expert talents, and pursue a purpose-driven life. The first was the attack on the World Trade Center (9/11). The second was the COVID-19 pandemic. They realized that winning the "rat race" meant they were still a rat, so many quit their jobs, relocated, ended relationships, or chose a modest lifestyle. We will show you how to develop and live a purpose-driven life in Part 3 of this book. In doing so, we hope to spare you from a moment of crisis brought on by a disaster. What we advocate here is a roadmap to getting to that realization early in life so the remainder of life is filled with joy, peace, meaning, and happiness.

Let us look at some ways to narrow down your list of passions and get to your version of success sooner. First, identify your values. Start by thinking about what is important to you. What do you value in life? Your passions should align with your values, so understanding what matters to you can help you identify the areas where you are most passionate.

Reflect on what brings you joy. Think about the activities and experiences that bring you the most joy and fulfillment. What do you look forward to doing in your free time? What gives you a sense of satisfaction? These are likely areas where you are passionate.

Consider your strengths. Your passions are often closely tied to your strengths and talents. Consider the areas where you excel and enjoy working in—these are likely areas where you are most passionate and those that make you smile. If you smile just thinking about something, that may be a passion.

By trying new things, you may discover a passion you did not know you had. Allow yourself to explore different areas and see what resonates with you. Remember, you do not know what you do not know, so be open to the unknown pleasure of something new and take the time to learn about different areas of interest. This can help you better understand what it takes to pursue a passion and determine if it is something you want to pursue further.

Pay attention to your feelings. As you engage in activities, pay attention to how you feel. Do you feel excited? Do you lose track of time? These are signs that you may be passionate about the activity.

It is important to note that passions can evolve and change over time. As you grow and develop, you may discover new passions or lose interest in previous ones, so remember it is okay to be flexible and open to new experiences. Although you may not be ready to develop goals for your adult life, you still need to learn how to develop your goals and set mini-goals as you go. We will help you do this in Chapter 12. The better version of goal setting is called SMART goal setting. We will take you through what it means and how to develop yours.

Differentiating between Skills and Passions

As you narrow down your list of passions, you must differentiate further between your skills and your passions. While your skills and talents may be important in pursuing your passions, they are not the same thing.

I created a model for assessing skills that fall into four categories. First, we look at skills you are good at and like using. Second, we look at skills you are good at but dislike using. Third, we look at skills you are not good at but like using. Last, we look at skills you are not good at and dislike using. How many people are stuck in dead-in jobs they are not good at and hate? We will help you come to a clear revelation about the skills you love using and the possibility of finding a job that will pay you for them.

Sometimes, you must use skills you hate and cannot avoid them. So, we cover the necessity of adding those to your skills improvement plan, which we will cover in Chapter 10. Skills are things you are good at and have developed through practice and experience. Passions are things that make you smile just thinking about them—you will never stay in bed thinking about your passions because you cannot wait to enjoy them. Living a life of passion and purpose will allow you to sleep well at night, knowing you enjoyed the day and made a difference.

To further differentiate between your skills and passions, consider that passion is what excites you. Your passions are the things that give you joy and inspire you. They may not necessarily be things you are already skilled at, but you are naturally drawn to them. They may be things like music, travel, helping others, or social justice.

On the other hand, skills are the things you have developed through practice and experience, but they may not necessarily be things that you are passionate about. They may be things like repairing a car, speaking a foreign language, or writing.

Passion requires little motivation because when you are passionate about something, you do not need much motivation to pursue it. It is something you naturally enjoy and want to do. You may even take a low-paying job because you enjoy what you do.

While you may be naturally talented in certain areas, developing your skills usually requires learning and practice before someone will pay you for those skills. This may involve taking classes, seeking mentorship, or investing time and energy to develop your abilities. Some of you may be asking, what is the difference between talent and skill? After all, we spent Chapter 1 covering how to find your talents. Talent and skill are words often used interchangeably, but one key difference is how they are acquired. You are born with particular talents, whereas you can learn and master many skills. I also look at skills as those attributes companies are willing to pay for to achieve their goals. Companies generally do not care about your talents or passions, just your skills.

How Parents Can Help

Parents can also play a vital role in helping teenagers identify their passions. Let us review some crucial ways parents can help.

First, provide resources and support to help your children develop their skills and pursue their passions. This support may include enrolling them in classes or programs, providing access to materials and equipment, or connecting them with mentors. It could also include helping them get summer internships, where they get detailed skills training.

Next, pair them with role models who can offer guidance and coaching on a particular skill. We will cover how to do this in Chapter 7.

In addition, ask open-ended questions. Instead of asking yes or no questions, ask open-ended questions that encourage your children to think about their interests and passions. For example, instead of asking, "Do you like taking pictures with your phone?" ask, "Why do you enjoy taking pictures?" This can help your children articulate their thoughts and feelings about what they like and why they like it. Simon Sinek wrote a bestselling book called *The Golden Circle* that corporations use to teach leaders how to effectively develop more productive and happier employees. Parents can benefit from reading this book because it gets to the point of understanding why someone does something so you can get the best out of them.

Be a good listener when your children talk about their interests and passions and show interest and enthusiasm for what they are saying. While supporting your children's passions is important, it is also essential to encourage balance. Help your children prioritize their commitments and activities so they have time for their passions and other important aspects of their lives, such as schoolwork, family time, social activities, and chores.

By providing these types of support and guidance, parents can help their children identify and enjoy their passions, leading to greater fulfillment and success in life. The greatest defense against depression is enjoying what you do. People have said they escape anxiety and stress by engaging in their passions, even if only for a little while.

Key Takeaways

In this chapter, we covered a lot about passion and how to identify and enjoy passions. We touched on the definition of passion and how it motivates us. We showed the difference between talents, passions, and skills and referred you to Chapter 10 for help with developing your skills. We gave several tips to try and reminded you that if you do what you love, you will not have much stress. Although we gave examples of how parents can help, the next chapter will focus more on parents and passion.

Your Next Steps

We know you highlighted a lot of points in this chapter. Identifying passions is a challenging exercise for many people. That is why we included a "Skills to Passion Assessment Model" at the end of this book. Get your mentor or parent to help you with completing this model.

It may seem complicated, but it works. Start with your talents from your Chapter 1 list, identify passions from that list, identify skills that enable those passions, identify job titles that require those skills, and then identify companies that offer those good-paying jobs. Okay, that does seem complicated—you may need to ask your school guidance counselor for help with that one.

Another great resource is SCORE, the Service Corps of Retired Executives. This volunteer group of retired experts helps people with business skills and development guidance.

In the next chapter, you will learn why parents are vital in identifying your passions and building your confidence.

Chapter 4 – Parents, Passion, and Confidence

"There is no such thing as a perfect parent. So just be the best one you can be". "Parenting is the easiest thing in the world to have an opinion about, but the hardest thing in the world to do." Matt Walsh

In the last chapter, we discussed how to identify and enjoy your passions, how to avoid getting stuck in life, and how to clarify what you enjoy. We also pointed out how to separate passions from your list of talents so you can focus on your purpose in life. Many people get skills, talents, and passions confused, so we took time to differentiate them. We ended the chapter by pointing out how parents can help their children identify their passions.

In this chapter, we expand on the role of parents in building confidence and self-esteem. Without a solid foundation of confidence and self-esteem, children may not engage in this new journey willingly or may not participate in the activities recommended. We will explore why parents' involvement in their children's passions is essential and how they can effectively support their children. Parents play a crucial role in shaping their children's lives, including their interests, talents, and passions, so helping children discover and pursue their passions is not only fulfilling for the child but also necessary for their overall development and success. Confident children make parents smile.

Question: What knowledge or skills do parents need to coach and advise a teenager on success?

What happened to the days when elders passed down knowledge and wisdom to new generations within the family? Too many people skip the family reunion or delay asking Grandma what she learned over the years. Successful adults must give back to younger generations by sharing their experiences and knowledge, and this is not accomplished by judging and complaining but by providing methods and tips for achieving success.

All parents want to give their children lots of attention and have them grow up believing they can achieve more than the past generation. Too often, parents work long hours and demanding jobs, so energy for the kids may be in short supply when they get home. Part of the challenge is that every parent is new at raising a child and doing it for the first time. We all learn by trial and error, hoping to do an excellent job, and most would assert they did the best they could, given the circumstances. The circumstances are complex and vary from one parent to the next.

Parents are the primary influencers in a child's life. They play a vital role in shaping their values, beliefs, and attitudes. As children grow, parents can help them discover their passions by encouraging exploration and providing opportunities to try new things, as discussed in Chapter 1. Children are more likely to develop passions when they feel supported and encouraged.

When parents support their children's passions, they also give them a sense of purpose and direction. This can lead to improved self-esteem, increased motivation, and a greater sense of well-being. Some teenagers struggle to figure out who they are and what is important to them, and their identity can be distorted by their parents who wanted a particular lifestyle. Transferring a parent's desired style to a child may backfire and negatively affect them. Children who know who they are and have a sense of purpose are more likely to achieve their goals and succeed in school and other areas of life.

Considerations for Parents

Here are reasons why it is so vital for parents to be involved in their children's development and passions.

When children are allowed to explore their interests and passions, they are more likely to develop a keen sense of self-identity. They better understand who they are and what they like and value, leading to increased self-confidence and resilience. This helps them make good decisions.

When children pursue their passions, they experience a sense of purpose and fulfillment, which contributes to their overall mental health and well-being. Passion also helps children manage stress and anxiety and build positive coping mechanisms. People who follow strong passions daily to make money will likely not experience hopelessness.

When children are passionate about their learning, they are more engaged and motivated, often leading to improved academic performance. If they connect what they are learning to a skill needed to pursue their passion, they will learn more effectively and willingly.

Pursuing passions can also help children develop better social skills, including communication, collaboration, and teamwork. When children are involved in activities they enjoy, they are more likely to build positive relationships and connections with others who share their interests, and this allows them to differentiate those who add value from those who lead them to mischief.

Parents need to listen to their children and encourage them to pursue what they are passionate about without pushing them in a particular direction. Parents can show interest and support for their children's passions by attending their events or performances, helping them practice or improve, and providing the necessary resources or equipment. Children will always look for a parent at their event and be disappointed when they are missing.

It is also important for parents to allow their children to pursue their passions independently, without hovering or micromanaging. Parents can emphasize the importance of balance, helping children understand that while pursuing their passions is essential, so is taking care of their health, relationships, and responsibilities.

Parents Be Careful

While parents can positively impact their children's passion development, they can also inadvertently hinder it. Here are some mistakes parents might make when falling short of this responsibility.

Parents may be tempted to encourage their children to pursue their own interests rather than allowing their children to explore and develop their own passions. This can pressure children to pursue activities they may not enjoy or be passionate about. Remember, a parent should not live vicariously through their children because they may not want what you want. An example of this is forcing a child to attend the parent's college instead of allowing the child to go with their friends to a different school.

Parents may also unintentionally discourage their children from pursuing their passions by being overly critical or dismissive of their interests. For example, some children know early in life that sports are not for them, and if parents push sports anyway, this can lead to children feeling unsupported and discouraged from pursuing their goals.

Parents may not give their children enough opportunities to explore different activities and interests. This can limit their children's exposure to various experiences and prevent them from discovering new passions. In Chapter 1, we covered how nonprofits and churches can help cover the cost of some activities or have programs tailored for exploration. Most

Boys & Girls Clubs and the YMCA have membership fees tied to the parents' financial capability, and these organizations provide excellent opportunities.

Finally, parents may ignore their children's interests altogether, failing to recognize the importance of allowing children to pursue their passions. This may happen when parents work extra hours or are stressed with other issues. After all, many parents never learned how to find their own passions and are living day-to-day in a state of despair. You can choose a better way for your children and give them a chance at happiness and purpose while making a decent living.

Dads Get Lots of Blame

It is often said that dads were given a short supply of patience. Some men take the heat for their lack of emotional support, but they sometimes have good reasons for not being emotionally supportive. Some males are taught to hide their emotions, avoid sharing deep feelings, and not seek feedback. Some women make fun of men who share too much emotion, and they think it is a sign of weakness. However, some men carry a huge burden and may not have an environment where they can let it out, so they hold it in until it gets released to the children or the spouse.

The 21st century has many examples of young men committing to do better and be more attentive to their children. Experts are clear that emotional development starts with infants. Without the warm embrace of their parents, an infant may show signs of underdevelopment. They may learn slower and call for attention less. Rejection is learned early in life, and we carry those insecurities into adulthood.

Aside from the impact of some fathers, there are many reasons why some Americans have less confidence or low self-esteem. Too many children were told to keep quiet and not run around the home. They could not get loud during play time and often could not interrupt a parent's time after a hard day's work. This treatment is traumatizing and may lead to anti-social behavior. Teachers observe a lack of parental involvement at school or a lack of support with homework.

Although blaming parents is tempting, many work two or three jobs. Throughout it all, children seem to bear the brunt of a lack of attention. Therefore, any discussion about success must include being honest with children because they already feel and see the efforts of their disorganized development. By reading this book, children and parents can be assured there is a path to success, even if their parents are learning along the way.

Keep Hope Alive

If this all seems too familiar, have hope because there is good news. New mothers and fathers are learning how to be great parents. They take classes and read books to learn what to do and what not to do, and there are videos everywhere that coach parents on building confidence and self-esteem in their children. Most states have healthcare programs for children, and schools have resource personnel who specialize in students with sadness or despair.

I can write about these things because I have children of my own. I know that boys and girls have unique needs. I also know that kids do not understand when a father is always busy, regardless of the reason. Children may not remember every time a father was present at an event, but they always remember when they were missing. Their need for love and attention is built into their DNA.

One of my daughters was always independent and smart. However, just because she did not need to ask lots of questions did not mean she needed to be left alone. I learned when she was seven years old that I must learn new parenting techniques because what I learned growing up was not going to work with her.

My son was smart but quick to lose interest. It was not because he lacked interest; he learned quickly but got bored easily. I realized this when his grades improved from C's to A's and B's after we discussed his interest in computer programming. He told me he wanted to create video games, and when I explained he needed a college degree for that, he decided that was his goal. After that conversation, it was clear to him why he needed to learn subjects like math and writing. High school did not teach him what he wanted to know to fuel his passion. The adage "What is in it for me?" was on full display with him. He proved he had the capacity for greatness and simply needed a reason to dream bigger and a roadmap to get there.

I was also lucky to be married to a nurse who had worked in the medical industry for over three decades. She was patient, so I could learn by watching her.

Children blame parents for the mistakes they perceive were made, and parents sometimes blame children for not listening to their advice. The reality is both are struggling to adapt to something they may have never done before. All the parenting websites, training classes, and books, like this one, should help the current generation of children get a better shot at succeeding without learning it the hard way.

Key Takeaways

In this chapter, we covered a lot about passion, confidence, self-esteem, and parental support. We emphasized that children need to understand that their parents love them and want the best for them. Children can help by expressing their thoughts, passions, and desires in extended conversations with their parents.

We pointed out that parents must understand that their views may be outdated. Clinging to tradition is good in some ways but may not fit the 21st century. The need to complete a college degree is being challenged on many fronts, and how people earn money has been redefined in ways many parents cannot comprehend. Everyone in a family needs to accept and collaborate on the idea that we are in it together.

In the next chapter, we highlight the danger children and parents underestimate. Studies have shown that social media may give children an unrealistic view of life and success. It also risks replacing genuine relationships with fake ones, and let's face it, no one has 1,000 friends. Social behavior is being rewritten in front of us, and we seem not to be paying attention. Although there are positives associated with using social media, there are plenty of dangers. As you read the next chapter, do not simply understand the issue—do something different.

Your Next Steps

You may need a new yellow highlighter at this point because we covered a lot of great points. The action for parents is to understand that you were never given a "how to" book on being a parent. That means you must admit when you make mistakes and acknowledge you do not know everything about developing a child, and it also means you must seek out parents who do a better job or have better outcomes. There is nothing wrong with getting expert advice, and your child will be better because of it. Put aside your pride and realize the world is changing fast.

The action for teenagers is to understand that parents are doing the best they can and want the best outcome. You should be more open to longer, deeper, more engaging conversations.

The action for parents is to read the book *The Golden Circle* by Simon Sinek to understand why people do things. Parents should look for two classes on communications: The first one is effective listening, and the second is communicating with a purpose. Both of these classes will help you understand what your teenager is communicating to you and help you communicate with them more clearly.

Chapter 5 – Beware of Social Media

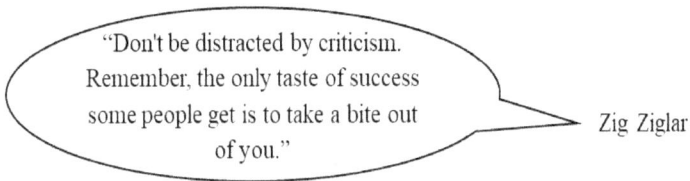

"Don't be distracted by criticism. Remember, the only taste of success some people get is to take a bite out of you." — Zig Ziglar

Although we recommended social media to showcase your talent in Chapter 2, be mindful of the disadvantages. Social media has become integral to your life, providing a platform for communication, entertainment, and self-expression. However, there are also risks and challenges associated with social media use, and you and your parents need to be aware of these and take steps to minimize the negative impacts.

This chapter will explore some of the potential risks of social media, including cyberbullying, data and personal privacy concerns, and the negative impact on mental health and self-esteem. It will also guide you on how to stay safe on social media, including adjusting your privacy settings, being mindful of the content you share, and avoiding risky behavior online.

Additionally, we will explore the impact of social media on relationships, including how it can lead to social isolation, create misunderstandings, and impact communication skills. This chapter will provide tips for maintaining healthy relationships while using social media, such as balancing online and offline interactions and avoiding over-reliance on social media for friends.

Some people have the illusion of having friends on social media, and I have heard people say they have hundreds of friends on social media. The reality is that if we have five good friends, we are blessed, and you must develop authentic relationships and interact with people in person. We will discuss the importance of a core group of friends in Chapter 13.

Question: As you think about your "friends list" on social media, how many of those would help you if you put out an urgent need for support?

By providing a comprehensive overview of the risks and challenges associated with social media, this chapter aims to help you and your parents make informed decisions about how to engage with social media in a safe and healthy way.

The Advantages of Social Media

Social media can help with increased visibility. Sharing your passions on social media can help you reach a wider audience and increase your visibility. This can be especially helpful if you are trying to build a personal brand or attract attention to your work.

Social media can provide a platform for you to connect with others who share your passions. This can help you build a sense of community and find like-minded individuals who can offer support and encouragement. You may learn from those with skills and talents that align with your own.

By sharing artistic work or ideas on social media, you can receive feedback from a diverse range of people. This can help you improve your skills and refine ideas. However, keep in mind that some feedback will not be good or intended to help you—the quote at the beginning of this chapter shows that some people love being negative on social media. Shaming, bullying, and rudeness are common reasons for anxiety and depression.

The Disadvantages of Social Media

Cyberbullying is a major issue on most platforms and is arguably getting worse. Unfortunately, social media can also be a platform for attacks and threats, and sharing your passions on social media may make you more vulnerable to negative comments or harassment. Some people have extremely low self-esteem and show it by bringing you down.

On the other hand, seeing others' successes and accomplishments on social media can lead to comparison and feelings of inadequacy. Because of that, social media may cause issues with self-esteem. You may feel pressure to keep up with others, look a certain way, or worry that your work is not good enough.

Sharing personal information on social media can also raise privacy and safety concerns. You may inadvertently share too much information or become vulnerable to online predators.

You and your parents must weigh the pros and cons of sharing passions, thoughts, and activities on social media and take steps to minimize the risks. This might include adjusting your privacy settings, being selective about what you share, and monitoring your social media activity for signs of cyberbullying or other harmful behavior. Remember, just because they are on your friends' list does not mean they are your friends.

How Parents Can Help

Parents, you can play a crucial role in coaching your children on how to use social media properly and how to deal with the potential risks and disadvantages that come with it. Let's review a few things that might help.

It is vital for you, as a parent, to establish clear rules and expectations around social media use, including how much time your children can spend online, what types of content are appropriate to share, and how to handle negative interactions or cyberbullying. Discussing these rules with your children openly and regularly reviewing them as needed is best.

You should educate your children on how to protect their privacy and security online. This includes setting strong passwords, using two-factor authentication, and being mindful of what they share online. You should also encourage your children to report all suspicious activity or interactions online. When they do report it, do not overreact, and if they make a mistake, focus on teaching them and encourage open conversation. An adverse reaction will only guarantee that your child will not open up to you again about their online activity.

While it is important to respect children's privacy, you should also monitor your children's social media activity to ensure they are using it safely and appropriately. This might include periodically checking their profiles, inspecting their direct messages, setting up parental controls, and monitoring who is on their friend list.

Children need to have a healthy balance between online and offline activities. Encourage your children to engage in other activities, such as sports, hobbies, or spending time with real friends and family.

Unfortunately, negative interactions on social media are common. You should teach your children how to handle these interactions by blocking or reporting the person and seeking support from a trusted adult. By providing guidance, education, and support, you can help your children use social media safely and healthily and minimize the potential risks.

Key Takeaways

In this chapter, we dealt head-on with the dangers of using social media. It can be used for good, but not everyone wants to be helpful. There are too many suicides associated with bullying on social media, so parents must be diligent in their efforts to coach their children. We covered the advantages, disadvantages, and provided ways you, as a parent, can help.

We hope you take careful notes of your plan for the proper role of social media.

We have covered all the chapters in Part 1 of this book, dealing with finding your talents and passions. So, we now change topics and will cover Part 2: Preparing for Success. We will start with Chapter 6, which covers assessing your strengths and weaknesses. We mentioned earlier that we would cover a model for evaluating skills, so prepare for a different way of doing it.

Your Next Steps

Think carefully about how you use social media and what you share. To do so, take inventory of your actions and decide what needs to change, and then write down what you should continue and what you will stop doing on social media. If social media is not helping you grow and be happier, it is not a place for you. You would not stay at an unhealthy or dangerous party, so why is social media any different?

As parents, you must learn what social media is and how your children use each platform. That means you must dig deeper and learn how to set security parameters. Also ensure no older adults you do not know are in your child's friends list. It would help if you put a reminder on your calendar to engage with your child about their experience on social media and how it makes them feel. Remember, you are the guardian of the gate for the safety and security of your children, and that includes social media more than ever because dangers abound on every platform.

Part 2

Preparation Enables Success

PART 2 | Preparation Enables Success

"One important key to success is self-confidence. An important key to self-confidence is preparation".

Arthur Ashe

Michael Jordan's preparation to become the greatest basketball player was a long and hard journey. From a young age, he showed an intense passion for basketball and spent countless hours practicing his skills. Jordan's work ethic was legendary; he often stayed on the court long after his teammates had gone home. This hard work made him the greatest basketball player of all time.

Before we discuss how to get and assess skills that support your passion, let us revisit what skills are and why they are essential. Skills refer to the abilities and expertise you acquire through training, practice, and experience, enabling you to perform specific tasks effectively. Skills can be broadly categorized into hard skills, which are specific to a particular job or field, and soft skills, which are more interpersonal and communication abilities. Many have argued that soft skills are not getting enough attention because soft skills, including communication, teamwork, and interacting with others, are vital in interpersonal relationships and collaborative work environments. Strong communication skills, for example, enable individuals to express ideas clearly, work with others effectively, and build positive relationships.

The acquisition and utilization of skills require you to put in the hard work. Lots of people have dreams, but many people fail because they become complacent. Denzel Washington once said, "Dreams without work are just dreams." Putting in the work is an enabler to achieving your dreams. Michael Jordan was the best because he worked hard every day to improve his skills. Before revealing Tiger Woods to the world of golf, his father "made" him do the work first. Richard Williams ensured that his daughters, Venus and Serena Williams, worked hard before declaring they could win the US Open Tennis Championship. Michael, Tiger, and Serena speak often about putting in the hard work to enable success.

In Part 1 of this book, we covered talents and passions. In Part 2, we focus on preparing for the future and how preparation is a critical component of achieving success in life. The deliberate and systematic process of acquiring knowledge, skills, and experiences enables individuals to achieve their goals and objectives. Preparation helps individuals plan, organize, and execute their tasks effectively, efficiently, and confidently, and hard work identifies what you do well and what needs improvement. Therefore, do not take shortcuts on your personal training and practicing of your skills.

Preparation enables success in several ways. First, it allows individuals to identify their strengths and improve their weaknesses. Their efforts may involve formal education, training, or internships, and these help individuals become more self-aware, which is an essential component of success. Second, preparation allows individuals to develop the skills and knowledge to succeed in their chosen fields. (We will help you map skills to desired jobs later in Chapter 6.) Third, preparation helps individuals to anticipate challenges and obstacles they may encounter along the way. By planning ahead, individuals can develop strategies to overcome these challenges and stay on track toward achieving their goals.

In the following five chapters of Part 2, we will cover the following topics.

- ✓ Assess your strengths and weaknesses
- ✓ Identify your success team
- ✓ Decide how you want feedback
- ✓ Learn from your mistakes
- ✓ Document your skills development plan

Chapter 6 – Assess Your Strengths and Weaknesses

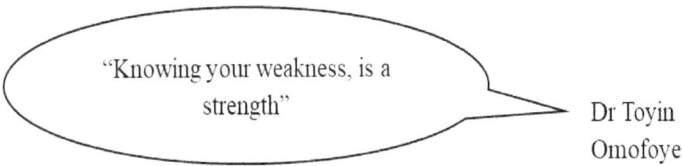

"Knowing your weakness, is a strength"

Dr Toyin
Omofoye

In this chapter, you will learn why assessing your strengths and weaknesses is vital before you start your development activities. This part of the book deals with preparation. So, to prepare, you need to know what you are good at and what talents you have that need development.

Success is not just about finding your passion or developing the right skills—it is also about knowing yourself and understanding your strengths and weaknesses. You may get immense joy from what you do well already; however, there may be talents that give you boundless joy even though you are disappointed you are not good at them. Imagine how much pleasure you could get if you improved those weaknesses and had multiple things that made you happy.

This chapter will explore the importance of assessing your strengths and weaknesses, how to do it, and how to use that knowledge to succeed.

Questions: What is your greatest strength, and what weakness do you think would stand out in your friends' minds?

Assessing your strengths and weaknesses is important for several reasons. First, it helps you identify your unique talents and abilities. By understanding what you are good at, you can focus your efforts on areas where you excel and achieve tremendous success. Additionally, it helps you identify areas where you need to improve. Acknowledging your weaknesses gives you the opportunity to develop new skills and improve where you fall short. Third, understanding your strengths and weaknesses helps you make better career decisions. With this knowledge, you can choose a career that fits your talents and passions and avoid career paths that may not be a good fit.

How to Assess Your Strengths and Weaknesses

Assessing your strengths and weaknesses can be challenging, but it is essential for achieving success. Let's review some steps to help you get started.

Start by reflecting on your experiences to assess your strengths and weaknesses. Think about the tasks or activities you enjoy and excel at. What do you like about them, and why are you good at them? On the other hand, think about the tasks or activities that you find challenging or struggle with. What do you find difficult about them, and why do you struggle with them? As we said in Chapter 1, you must explore lots of activities and talents to assess what you like and are good at.

There are several assessments that can help you identify your strengths and weaknesses. These may include personality tests, career assessments, and skills assessments, and they can provide valuable insights into your personality traits, interests, and abilities. While assessments may provide a helpful starting point, remember that they are just one tool in the process of assessing your strengths and weaknesses.

Back in Chapter 1, we mentioned two resources you might like. Gallup.com has an assessment that identifies your top five strengths based on your responses to a series of questions (CliftonStrengths n.d.). Similarly, the Myers-Briggs Type Indicator assessment by mbtionline.com helps you understand your personality type, including your strengths and weaknesses ("Official Myers-Briggs Test and Personality Assessment" n.d.). Both assessments are inexpensive and may fit teenagers and young adults well.

Feedback from others can be valuable in assessing your strengths and weaknesses. Ask your friends, family, and colleagues for feedback on your strengths and weaknesses because they may be able to provide insights you may not have considered. But be careful—not everyone wants to see you succeed. Jealousy and competition from some of your so-called friends could be powerful deterrents.

Keep track of your successes and failures. Some people enjoy noting these in their personal journals; keeping a journal could help you identify patterns in your behavior and areas where you need to improve. Record your achievements and challenges and identify the skills and qualities that contributed to those outcomes.

We wrote about the benefits of competition in Part 1. Success and failure are best tested by competition in school events or outside programs. Once you have identified your strengths and weaknesses, the next step is to use that knowledge to plan for improvement. Let's cover some ways to do that.

First, identify your top strengths and find ways to use them to your advantage. This may involve seeking opportunities that allow you to use your strengths or finding ways to apply your strengths to tasks or projects that you may not have considered before. For example, volunteering at a nonprofit is a wonderful way to use talents and skills safely. Some organizations will train you on the task at hand.

Next, identify your top weaknesses and find ways to improve them. This may involve taking classes or courses, seeking mentorship or coaching, or finding ways to practice and develop your skills. To help with this, we included a developmental action plan in the back of this book, so use it to plan your improvement over the coming months. Also, do not forget to include your family and friends in this discussion and get their recommendations.

Balance is critical to achieving success. While focusing on your strengths and developing your weaknesses is important, you must also recognize that you cannot be good at everything, nor do you get joy from doing too many things you are good at. Focus on areas where you excel, but also recognize the value of collaboration and working with others who have complementary skills. The key is to prioritize your passions while balancing the necessities of life.

Use your knowledge of your strengths and weaknesses to set realistic goals for yourself. Identify areas where you want to improve and set specific, measurable goals to help you achieve those improvements. Do not try to be perfect—instead, focus on getting better. Remember, practice does not make perfect, but practice does make progress.

In Chapter 3, we covered the difference between skills and passions. Let us look at skills as they relate to enabling you to enjoy your talents and passion. The idea is to never be depressed about your life's journey or at least live a life of joy and purpose. Some jobs require skills you may hate using but are necessary to make money, and part of your new way of thinking is to see skills as useful only if they help you pursue your passions or are required for a particular career choice.

Skills and the Economic Cycle You Are Living In

Before you can identify and assess the core skills you need to use, you first need to recognize the economic cycle you live in. You see, skills are aligned with how people make money. There was a time when parents could pass down skills and children could succeed based on these skills. The 21st century reminds us that technology and economic cycles change too quickly for that to work today. Some teenagers know what they want to learn in college, but those skills may be obsolete by the time they graduate. So, how can you navigate this problem and prevent putting yourself in a trap before you can execute your plan? The answer is modeling future shifts in how people make money.

For you to see this more clearly, I need to get into some details about the past 2,000 years of change. We will cover the details of world economic cycle changes in Chapter 14, which will tie it to why you must continuously learn new skills. For now, let us stick with the skills we identified that will fuel our passions and help us make money.

Let's Assess Some Skills

To live your dream of getting paid for using your passions, you will need help with two models. First, you need to identify your skills honestly. That means opening up and being honest about your view of self and others' view of you. Second, you must map your essential passion-driven skills with a job that pays the bills.

We created a model for assessing skills that will tie directly to your passions and the type of life you want to live. Our "Passion to Skills Assessment Model" in Figure 2 below shows four quadrants with questions. This simple model is powerful in that it will get you to see what you want to spend your life doing, and it helps you focus on skills you avoid because you do not like doing them. Although you may not like using some of those skills, reality may require you to be good at them to complete tasks in your job or business.

Figure 2

**Passion to Skills
Assessment Model**

What skills do you like using and are good at?	What skills do you like using but are not good at?
Enter your response	Enter your response
Practice and sell these skills.	Add these skills to your improvement plan.
What skills do you dislike using but are good at?	What skills do you dislike using and are not good at?
Enter your response	Enter your response
Tolerate these skills because they are necessary	Some skills are needed, so add them to your improvement plan. Others can be ignored.

Remember that natural talents are something you are good at from birth. Skills, on the other hand, are necessary for daily living or performing tasks companies will pay you to do. While you may need to develop some skills you have no passion for, they are still necessary. Think of tasks like doing spreadsheets or filling out expense reports, which most people dislike but are required for many jobs. Similarly, doing repairs around the house is necessary, even though most people dislike doing them.

Here are the questions from the Passion to Skills Assessment Model that you must answer honestly. Completing the form requires you to be vulnerable and possibly uncomfortable.

The first question in Quadrant 1 is: What skills do you **like using** and are **good at?**

The question in Quadrant 2 is: What skills do you **like using** but are **not good at**?

The question in Quadrant 3 is: What skills do you **dislike using** but are **good at**?

The question in Quadrant 4 is: What skills do you **dislike using** and are **not good at**?

Once you have the answers, you can smile. You now know what you like, what you are good at, and what you hate, and knowing these are necessary for life. Sounds simple, right? Use the blank "Passion to Skills Assessment Model" form at the back of this book and meet with your parent or mentor to complete it. Meeting with someone you trust will require digging deep and being honest with your answers. Do not do this with someone you work with unless you trust the answers will not get back to your boss. Once you are done, you can map skills you can sell to a hiring manager or add weaknesses to your skills improvement action plan. You can sell those new skills to get that dream job one day.

We also created a Skills to Jobs Mapping Model below to help you map your preferred skills to a career or job title. We included a blank sample at the back of this book so you can complete your map with the help of your family or mentor. All our forms and figures are available on our website, so you can also fill them out electronically. Download a copy of the documents at dare2succeed.org. We show a sample in Figure 3 below so you see how this works, but your form will look different based on your input.

Figure 3

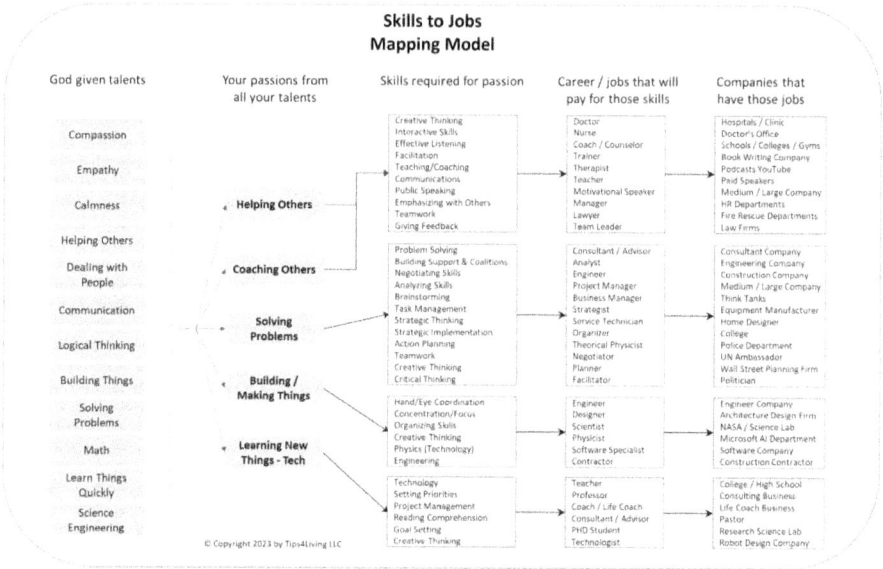

Skills to Jobs Mapping Model

God given talents	Your passions from all your talents	Skills required for passion	Career / jobs that will pay for those skills	Companies that have those jobs
Compassion		Creative Thinking	Doctor	Hospitals / Clinic
		Interactive Skills	Nurse	Doctor's Office
Empathy		Effective Listening	Coach / Counselor	Schools / Colleges / Gyms
		Facilitation	Trainer	Book Writing Company
	Helping Others	Teaching/Coaching	Therapist	Podcasts YouTube
Calmness		Communications	Teacher	Paid Speakers
		Public Speaking	Motivational Speaker	Medium / Large Company
Helping Others		Emphasizing with Others	Manager	HR Departments
		Teamwork	Lawyer	Fire Rescue Departments
Dealing with People	Coaching Others	Giving Feedback	Team Leader	Law Firms
		Problem Solving	Consultant / Advisor	Consultant Company
Communication		Building Support & Coalitions	Analyst	Engineering Company
		Negotiating Skills	Engineer	Construction Company
Logical Thinking	Solving Problems	Analyzing Skills	Project Manager	Medium / Large Company
		Brainstorming	Business Manager	Think Tanks
Building Things		Task Management	Strategist	Equipment Manufacturer
		Strategic Thinking	Service Technician	Home Designer
Solving Problems	Building / Making Things	Strategic Implementation	Organizer	College
		Action Planning	Theorical Physicist	Police Department
		Teamwork	Negotiator	UN Ambassador
Math		Creative Thinking	Planner	Wall Street Planning Firm
	Learning New Things - Tech	Critical Thinking	Facilitator	Politician
Learn Things Quickly		Hand/Eye Coordination	Engineer	Engineer Company
		Concentration/Focus	Designer	Architecture Design Firm
		Organizing Skills	Scientist	NASA / Science Lab
Science		Creative Thinking	Physicist	Microsoft AI Department
		Physics (Technology)	Software Specialist	Software Company
Engineering		Engineering	Contractor	Construction Contractor
		Technology	Teacher	College / High School
		Setting Priorities	Professor	Consulting Business
		Project Management	Coach / Life Coach	Life Coach Business
		Reading Comprehension	Consultant / Advisor	Pastor
		Goal Setting	PHD Student	Research Science Lab
		Creative Thinking	Technologist	Robot Design Company

© Copyright 2023 by Tips4Living LLC

Most teenagers or parents may not know which companies offer jobs that align with specific skills. That is why using a mentor who understands different industries and job requirements is essential. This process requires you to have a business mentor on your success team—we will cover your success team in Chapter 7 so you understand why having different mentors is so important. No single mentor can help you with everything because no one has expertise in everything. By now, you can appreciate having someone who can guide you in developing your talents and passions. A different mentor can help you with your skills development and training based on their experience. Another mentor might focus on financial matters, and so on.

Once you understand the talents God gave you at birth and recognize which talents provide you with joy, you see what your passions are, as we covered in Part 1. Now, you see how to map skills aligned with your passions so you can map a career or job to those passions. The last step is identifying companies that will pay you to use those skills and are respectful of your passion. Some organizations rank large companies based on their treatment of employees, so be sure to consider that.

One source of knowledge for this task is the nonprofit SCORE, which covers all types of business issues (SCORE n.d.). It stands for Service Corps of Retired Executives, and they partner with the small business administration to offer its business support services for free. Their volunteers provide business mentorships, local workshops, webinars, and various events in your area.

Assessing your strengths and weaknesses is an essential part of achieving success. By understanding your unique talents and abilities and areas where you need to improve, you can make better decisions about your career path and focus on areas that will make you happy throughout your career.

Key Takeaways

In this chapter, we covered the importance of assessing your strengths and weaknesses. We reviewed how to do an assessment using two inexpensive website resources. We also introduced you to a skills-to-passion assessment model and a skills-to-job mapping model our company created. We reminded you how critical it is to get feedback from those who experience your talents, passions, and skills. Although we mentioned setting goals and making a skills development plan after your assessment, those two topics require more explanation. So, we will cover goals in Chapter 12 and help you with the development action plan in Chapter 10.

The next chapter will focus on the importance of a "success team." We will show you how to identify three to five people for your team and get buy-in from parents and mentors. In addition, we will suggest how to plan coaching sessions and how often they should occur. Lastly, we ask you to decide how you want feedback in Chapter 8 because your team will need to know your preference to communicate effectively.

Your Next Steps

Meet with your mentor or parent and complete the Passion to Skills Assessment Model illustrated in Figure 2 above. Transfer skills in the right two boxes to your personal development plan so you can improve those skills.

Meet with your business mentor and complete the Skills to Jobs Mapping Model illustrated in Figure 3 above. This exercise will show how selecting your dream job is tied to your preferred skills that align with your passion, and this clarity will make decision-making easier when you get out of high school or college or even change your lifestyle later in life.

In the next chapter, you will decide who to go to for advice.

Chapter 7 – Identify Your Success Team

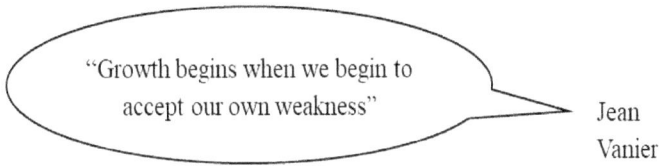

"Growth begins when we begin to accept our own weakness"

Jean Vanier

In the last chapter, we covered how to assess your strengths, weaknesses, and skills. We introduced two models to help you with this challenging process and mentioned how important your mentors will be in assisting you. Let us focus more on what a "success team" is and how you can use one to ensure your development and success.

In this chapter, we will define a success team and recommend several types of mentors for that team.

Question: Do you have people who can give you advice and feedback? If so, how have they helped you?

You Don't Know What You Don't Know

The first step in understanding how mentors can help you is acknowledging that you do not know everything. You are reading this book because you want answers and ideas for gaining success. Now is the time to put your ego aside, get a beverage, and open your mind to the possibility of "cheating the system." What I mean by that is gaining experience without experiencing something on your own. Someone else has already been there and done that, so why fail when you can get knowledge from someone who has failed and learned? That is the "cheat sheet" of life. If you want to be rich, you have to hang around rich people.

Mentors and Advisors

A mentor is an experienced and trusted advisor who provides guidance, support, and encouragement to a less experienced individual, a mentee. Mentors can help you be successful by providing you with a positive role model, helping you develop new skills, and offering guidance on life decisions. Mentors can have a significant impact on your life, leading to healthier relationships, lifestyle choices, better attitudes about others, enhanced self-esteem and self-confidence, and improved work performance. Mentors can help you develop communication, problem-solving, decision-making, and goal-setting skills, and they can provide you with feedback on your strengths and weaknesses and help you identify areas for improvement. You can learn more about mentoring at Youth.gov ("Benefits of Mentoring for Young People" n.d.).

Success Team

Now that your mind is open to what you do not know and you understand what mentoring is, let's understand who should be on your mentor team. I recommend you have five members on your advisory team, and I will list them below and explain what you want from each one. Before you read any further, I need you to admit that you do not know much about the world at your age. That is why getting feedback and input from those who have been there and done that is essential. The other thing you need to accept is that you probably hate to be criticized and told what to do. If you can accept that idea, you are ready.

Motivational/Spiritual Mentor – This person will help you discover who you are. This person will serve as your mirror as you develop your values, style, personality, principles, and behavior traits. They will confirm that your view of self is what other people see and recommend action when the two do not align. This person will help you with your talents, passions, and enjoyment of life. This person must be upbeat, optimistic, and one who does good for the sake of good.

Training and Development Mentor – This person will help you with your skills, training, and talent development. They will advise you on AP classes to take in high school and how to prepare for college. They will also help you align your skills with a career so you can live a life of joy while being paid for what you love. Think of teachers, trainers, and college development personnel for this role. Some people have teachers in their families, so this person should not be hard to find.

Business and Finance Mentor – This person will help you with managing money. They will ensure you have a FICA credit score above 700 and help you avoid common mistakes in managing debt and credit cards. They will ensure you understand "compound interest" and how this is the secret to building wealth while working. If you desire to start your own business, they will be your source of advice and coaching. Think of business owners, company managers, CPAs, or finance managers. Anyone with an MBA will meet the requirements.

Health and Wellness Mentor – This person should have expertise in healthy eating, fitness, and mental health wellness. Taking care of your body, mind, and soul is critical to living a life of purpose and passion, and stress, anxiety, and depression sometimes result from bad health, excess weight, or lack of peace. Think of nurses, doctors, therapists, dietitians, and personal gym trainers for this role.

Goals and Project Management Mentor – This person should have training or experience setting short and long-term goals. They will get deep into conversations about your goals and help you plan a course of action to achieve them. In addition, they will ensure you have a tracking method for each goal or mini-goal and follow up with you on getting them done. These mentors will help you balance everything you have to do and help organize and prioritize them. Think of program or project managers at work or people with skills in Microsoft Office software for tracking tasks.

Key Takeaways

In this chapter, we viewed what mentors are and how to use them. We recommended five roles for your "success team" and gave examples of experts to think about when picking your advisors. We cautioned you not to be cocky, let go of your ego, and accept the idea that you do not know much about the world. Others have been there and done that, so they can help you avoid mistakes and gain success much faster. In the next chapter, we will deal with that ego a bit more. Specifically, we will discuss why getting feedback is so important and how you can help your mentors by explaining your desired form of feedback.

Your Next Steps

Discuss your team of mentors with your parents or best friend, then select your mentors. Complete the "success team" mentor list form in Figure 4 at the end of this book.

Figure 4

Success Team Mentor List

Role	Responsibilities	Mentor Name	Mentor Experience	Feedback Method
Motivational & Spiritual Mentor	This person will help you with finding out who you are. As you develop your values, style, personality, principles and behavior traits, this person will serve as your mirror. They will confirm your view of self is what other people see and recommend action when the two don't align. This person will help you with your talents, passions and enjoyment of life. This person must be upbeat, optimistic and one who does good for the sake of good.			
Business & Finance Mentor	This person will help you with managing money. They will ensure you have a FICA credit score above 700 and help you avoid common mistakes for managing debt and credit cards. They will ensure you understand 'compound interest' and how this is the secret to building wealth while working. If you have a desire to start you own business, they will be your source of advice and coaching. Think of business owners, company managers, CPA's or finance managers. Anyone with an MBA will meet the requirements.			
Training & Development Mentor	This person will help you with your skills, training and talent development. They will advise you on AP classes to take in high school and prepare you for college. They will also help you align your skills with a career so you can live a life of joy, while being paid for what you love. Think of teachers, trainers and college development personnel for this role. Most people have teachers in their family, so this person shouldn't be hard to find.			
Health & Wellness Mentor	This person should have expertise in healthy eating, fitness and mental health wellness. Taking care of your body, mind and soul is critical to living a life of purpose and passion. Stress, anxiety and depression sometimes come as a result of bad health, excess weight or lack of peace. Think of nurses, doctors, therapists, dietitians, and personal gym trainers for this role.			
Goals & Project Management Mentor	This person should have training or experience with setting short and long term goals. They will get deep into conversations about your goals and help you plan a course of action to achieve them. They will make sure you have a tracking method for each goal or initiative and follow up with you on getting them done. They will help you balance all the stuff you have to do and help organize and prioritize them. Think of program/project managers at work or people with skills in Microsoft Office software for tracking tasks.			

Share the role definition above with each mentor and get their buy-in and agreement to fulfill that role.

In the next chapter, you will decide how you want feedback from your mentors, parents, and friends.

Chapter 8 – Decide How You Want Feedback

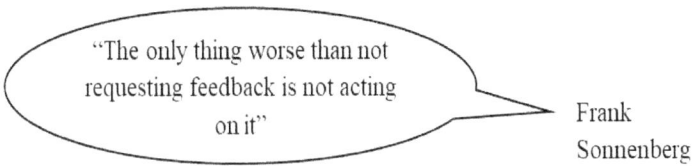

"The only thing worse than not requesting feedback is not acting on it"

Frank
Sonnenberg

In this chapter, we will discuss why feedback is important and why you need to know how you like to receive feedback. Getting feedback is essential for your success because it can help you improve your performance, increase your self-awareness, and identify areas for change. Feedback can provide valuable insights into your strengths and weaknesses, help you identify blind spots, and offer suggestions to add to your personal development plan.

Question: What method of feedback causes you to shut down?

Hearing Feedback Is Hard

Receiving feedback can be uncomfortable, but increasing self-awareness and growing personally and professionally is vital. You may feel any feedback is a criticism of you and how you do things, and you think you are good to go because your friends do not criticize you. But consider that most people are not willing to be honest with you because they want to keep the conversation positive and not upset you. Even your parents may walk a thin line when giving you bad news. After all, you may not take feedback well, and no one wants to be the one to tell you the truth. Bill Gates said, "We all need people who will give us feedback. That is how we improve." Bill became a billionaire in part because he knew the value of feedback.

Types of Feedback

Formal feedback, such as a quarterly evaluation session, is typically arranged and can be pre-planned. Informal feedback, on the other hand, is usually spontaneous and can happen at any time by text or phone call.

Peer-to-peer feedback is given by your friends, siblings, or coworkers and can be positive or negative. People use positive feedback to praise your behavior and provide encouragement, while negative feedback is used to identify areas for improvement or to make you feel bad.

Constructive feedback provides specific suggestions for improvement and is most effective in helping you succeed in life.

How Would You Like Your Dose of Feedback?

The way you handle feedback will directly tie to how you implement improvement. Therefore, you need to be comfortable with how you best handle bad news. Everyone can handle good news, but it is the bad news that sinks deep into our souls and creates emotions that may block comprehension. No two people handle bad news the same, so think about it. Get input from your friends and family and tell them to be honest with you. Once you have an idea of your preferred method, write it down.

It would help to express to each mentor how you want to get feedback. Also, tell them that they should include constructive feedback since growth and improvement are what they are on your team to do. Now, you are left to pick your feedback style. Do you need it in a formal or informal setting, planned or spontaneous, written or verbal? Knowing how you best receive bad news is essential for you to absorb the feedback and make changes.

At the very least, we suggest a quarterly planned session so you do not forget to share ideas for improvement. However, you should encourage your mentors to spontaneously provide you feedback on time-sensitive things—you do not want to make a wrong decision because your feedback session is two months away. Also, if need be, it would help if you called your mentor with questions and got input on life decisions. Last, do not forget about your parents. They should know what is going on with your decisions and the significant changes you are making.

Speaking with your parents before making decisions with your mentors is good practice. Then, circle back with your parents afterward.

Ways Parents Can Help

Encourage your child to speak honestly with you about their judgments. You should not judge them but focus instead on the act of constructive feedback. Respect that they must make their own decisions (if in high school or above). Parents should be involved with and approve the mentors assigned to the "success team" because your job is to protect them from adults you may not trust. So, you should recommend mentors and help them find experts willing to help. Do not forget that your extended family may have certified experts with lots of experience, so use them.

Key Takeaways

In this chapter, we discussed why feedback is essential and the different types of feedback. We asked you to let go of your ego and understand that good and bad feedback is necessary for your improvement. We asked you to decide how you want your feedback and write it down using the success team mentor form in Figure 4 above or at the back of this book. We gave suggestions for how parents can help.

Your Next Steps

Think through and decide how you want your feedback. With the help of your parents, decide who will be on your team and set up quarterly feedback sessions with each mentor so you do not miss any ideas.

On the form at the back of this book, write the name of each mentor, their role, the desired method of feedback, and the meeting schedule.

In the next chapter, you will learn why it is so critical to learn from your mistakes and how failure is the fuel for success.

Chapter 9 – Learn from Mistakes

"I can accept failure, everyone fails at something. But I can't accept not trying"

Michael Jordan

In this chapter, we will cover why failure and making mistakes are natural and cannot be avoided. Some people will beat themselves up after making mistakes or failing a task because they forget that everyone fails and no one is perfect. Sadness, stress, and depression sometimes occur because people cannot let go of the past, and it prevents them from moving forward. The famous book author J.K. Rowling once said, "It is impossible to live without failing at something unless you live so cautiously that you might as well not have lived at all, in which case you have failed by default."

Question: What specific example can you think of when you hesitated to do something for fear of making a mistake or failing?

If you cannot be perfect and will make mistakes, how can you use that to your advantage? The answer may lay in mathematics, where the statistics of chance and probability can be assured. Let me explain with a story from my past. My first experience with this was in college when I took a physics class. We had to guess how many heads would occur if you flipped a nickel.

I lost severely until I learned that the number of occurrences (n) affects the outcome. You see, if you flip a nickel four times, you have no idea if it will be head or tails. However, if you flip a nickel 100 times, you will get heads 50 times, plus or minus two. So, time and how many tries make a difference in the outcome.

If you want to succeed, you must fail before your chances are good and success is near. That leads us to another powerful secret: Do not be scared to try. Many people have great ideas but are afraid to start for fear of failing. The fear of failure is so powerful that many people talk themselves out of trying to avoid failing. I always tell my students, "For those afraid of failure, you should be more afraid of regret."

I am perplexed that people with an MBA degree will think they are not ready to start a business, so they go for a doctorate. Of course, you are better trained as a PHD, but that is not needed to start a business. Being 95% ready versus 80% ready is not a reason to defer your dreams—the idea is to acquire basic skills and go for it. It is amazing how passion can get you past the 20% you may not have learned already.

The Business Model for Success

Companies that sell products or services use what is called the "hit rate." To keep this short, that means if you knock on 10 doors, you will get two sales. That would be a 20% hit rate. They can then do a financial analysis by concluding that 1,000 sale calls will get 200 orders. Over time, experience will determine the hit rate for a particular company. Girl Scouts may also use this without knowing it—if they are in front of 500 people, they will likely get 100 sales for their cookies, at minimum. Their hit rate may be higher than the industrial average of 20%. Some scouts may be disappointed that 7 out of 10 people will say no to buying cookies. But the best sellers know that 3 out of every 10 people will say yes. Therefore, they only need to focus on increasing the number of people they are in front of to increase sales. I hope these examples clarify that you can be disappointed in the seven failures or motivated by the three successes. All right, enough of the complicated business science—let's look at more emotionally connected examples.

The Hero and Me

God gave everyone talents and skills. You may not know what you can succeed at because society tries hard to tell you who you should be and what you should do to earn a living. That brainwashing has run its course, and the 21st century is changing the rules too quickly for some to keep up with. Many are asking if a college degree is worth the return on investment, while others are facing hopelessness and despair and want a different way to succeed. This book is all about a different way to look at it, but first, I must convince you that you can succeed even after failure. You can be the hero of your family or community. Let us look at some examples to remind you that failure is the fuel to success.

Michael Jordan is remembered as a basketball superstar, a fierce competitor, and one of the best players in basketball history. However, he did not make the varsity team in his sophomore year of high school. Instead, he was placed on the junior varsity squad, which was a setback for the young athlete. The disappointment of not making the varsity team fueled Jordan's determination and motivated him to improve his game.

Oprah Winfrey faced a difficult, impoverished childhood and overcame numerous challenges to become a billionaire sensation. Her life story is an example of perseverance and resilience.

Thomas Edison is known for inventing the light bulb but famously said, "I have not failed. I've just found 10,000 ways that won't work." He encountered countless setbacks and made mistakes before getting it right.

Before founding Disney, Walt Disney faced many business failures and rejections. He was even fired from a newspaper job for lacking creativity and imagination. Yet, he went on to create one of the most iconic entertainment companies in the world and forged a legacy that most people are familiar with.

Albert Einstein, the renowned physicist, did not speak until he was four and did not read until he was seven. He faced academic difficulties and struggled to find a job early in his career. Nevertheless, his groundbreaking work in theoretical physics changed the world. Most physicists ground their work in Einstein's theories.

J.K. Rowling, the author of the Harry Potter series, faced rejection from multiple publishers before one finally accepted her manuscript. She went from living in poverty to becoming one of the world's wealthiest and most influential authors. Today, no one would believe that she failed at getting her first book accepted.

Colonel Harland Sanders, the founder of Kentucky Fried Chicken (KFC), did not find success until he was in his sixties. He started by using his social security checks. Before that, he faced multiple job failures and rejections.

The bestselling author Stephen King received numerous rejections for his early works. He even threw away the manuscript for his novel *Carrie* before it was eventually published, marking the start of his successful career. You can see that he almost gave up after throwing away that draft novel.

Do not let your fear of failure cause you to throw away your chance at success. Do it your way, on your terms, and be happy about how you choose to live a purpose-driven life. These individuals serve as inspirational examples of how persistence, determination, and learning from failure can lead to extraordinary success. Their stories remind you that setbacks and failures are often part of the path to achievement.

Remember, you were not born with all the answers, and you will make mistakes. That is part of being human, so embrace the mistakes and learn from them.

Key Takeaways

Now, you are fired up and motivated by the idea that you need to get on with failure so you can find your success. Let me remind you that the success you are after is living a life around your passion, for which someone will pay you so that you can be happy every day. By now, you know how to recognize your talents, identify your passions, map your skills to your dream job, and get training on your shortfalls. You have also identified the people who will serve as mentors and give you needed feedback, including the constructive feedback you need and even the feedback you may not want to hear.

Your Next Steps

Your only action is not to be afraid to do something. Nothing good will happen sitting on the couch. And if you fail at first, get up quickly and try again by learning from those mistakes.

In the next chapter, you will focus on improving your skills and ensuring that the skills you need are tied to how money is made in the 21st century.

Chapter 10 – Your Skills Improvement Plan

"There are no secrets to success. It is the result of preparation, hard work, and learning from failure"

Colin Powell

In the last chapter, we covered how failure is the fuel for success. You should not fear making mistakes but should thrive by learning from them. In this chapter, we will lay out a process for getting the skills you need to support your passion. Abraham Lincoln once said, "Give me six hours to chop down a tree, and I will spend the first four sharpening the ax." Skills improvement is not accidental—it is a plan of action.

Tying It All Together

In Chapter 1, we covered how to recognize and add your talents to your skills development plan to improve them. In Chapter 2, we covered how to showcase your abilities and add examples to your development plan to master them. In Chapter 3, we covered how to identify and enjoy your passions. Like talents, you must master the skills needed to support your passions. In Chapter 4, we covered how parents can help. Parents may identify skills that are necessary for success but may not be tied to a given passion. For example, good communication and public speaking are generic skills that everyone should have.

We wrapped up Chapter 5 by covering many aspects of social media. Some skills needed for interacting with the world are technology security, personal safety, and identity protection. You may not have thought of these skills in Chapter 5, but you definitely want to add them to your personal development plan now.

In Part 2, preparation enables success, and we started Chapter 6 by covering how to assess your strengths and weaknesses. I recap what we covered in these important chapters to remind you that your personal development plan should already have lots of items in it. In Chapter 7, your mentors may have thoughts about skills you need to add to prepare for a changing world. Although I referred to the form in the back of the book, let's take some time to review what a skills development plan is.

Question: What is the one thing you are not good at but want to be?

What Is a Personal Skills Development Plan?

A personal development plan (PDP) is a tool to help you achieve your goals in life, work, or education. It enables you to identify what you will learn, why, how, when, and what the skill connects with as a goal. A PDP can help you determine your skills, knowledge of a subject, and competency gaps and plan how to fill them with learning activities, feedback, or mentoring. Some of your learning may occur via YouTube, online workshops, college classes, and mentoring sessions. A PDP is an evergreen document, meaning it should change based on your goals. A PDP is not a one-time exercise but part of a lifelong, continuous learning lifestyle.

I include a sample PDP below in Figure 5 with common skills listed so you can see how the form works and how you should use it with your mentors.

Figure 5

Personal Development Plan

What – Skill	Why – reason for doing it	How – Activity To Improve	When – Due Date	Where – Method	Status
Public Speaking Skill	Communicate with confidence	Complete Toastmasters	June 2024	Local Church	Pending
Effective Listening Skill	To understand another person's needs	Complete an online class	July 2024	LinkedIn online classes	Pending
Coaching others	Provide ideas and support to others	Complete Life Coaching Certification	August 2024	Online website	Pending
Negotiating Skill	To be able to agree on difficult issues	Complete an online class	September 2024	LinkedIn online classes	Pending
Facilitation Skill	Facilitate others to agreement on issues	Complete an online class	October 2024	LinkedIn online classes	Pending
Presentation Software	Present ideas to others in meetings	Complete a Microsoft PowerPoint class	November 2024	Microsoft online learning	Pending
Finance Skills	Manage money successfully	Complete multiple classes on finance	December 2024	Nonprofit Workshops	Pending
Writing Skills	Be able to write a book or podcast	Complete classes on writing	March 2025	Book writers' club online	Pending
Team Player Skills	Work as a team member to achieve goals	Complete interactive skills class online	July 2025	LinkedIn online classes	Pending
Computer Skills	Use a computer well to achieve tasks	Complete a computer user class	August 2025	Nonprofit Workshops	Pending

Connecting Your PDP with Your Purpose-Driven Lifestyle

Documenting your PDP helps you define the kind of person you want to be, the skills you want to master, and the goals you want to achieve. Then, you map out your long and short-term goals to realize these desires and set due dates for when you want to reach your goals. We cover goals in Chapter 12, so hang in there. I offer digital versions of the documents at the back of the book on our website, so feel free to download your free copy as a courtesy for buying this book.

Key Takeaways

In this chapter, we covered what personal development (PDP) is and how you should use it. We reminded you of the items you should have jotted down from Chapter 1 through 6. If you do this exercise early in life, you may have many pages of items. Some items may require you to take a college class, while others can be done on LinkedIn, YouTube, or other online websites. This gives you the flexibility to complete courses as you desire without waiting for high school or college.

Your parents must also be involved in this exercise. Both of you may find that attending college is a great idea, or you may agree that you have an alternative to pursuing a life of purpose without a college degree. I am a big proponent of getting a college degree because that experience helps some teenagers transition to adulthood. However, I do recognize that some may find their college degree useless due to a quickly changing world.

Your Next Steps

Teenagers, parents, and mentors must work together to develop a personal development plan. Remember, perfection is a flaw, so do not waste time perfecting your strategy. The most important thing is identifying the skills you find necessary and getting started quickly on learning them. Learning is a lifelong pursuit, and you should never stop learning. I will spend considerable time explaining why continuous learning is critical in Chapter 14. Do not forget to add a review date on your calendar so you can inspect your progress with your mentors and update your status for each item.

Now that you have a better view of your talents, passion, skills, and the type of jobs you want, let's shift in Part 3 to developing a purpose-driven lifestyle.

Part 3

Live a Purpose-Driven Life

PART 3 | Live a Purpose Driven Life

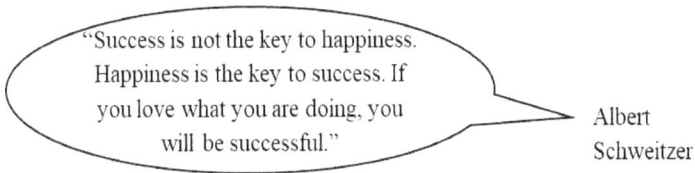

"Success is not the key to happiness. Happiness is the key to success. If you love what you are doing, you will be successful."

Albert Schweitzer

Martin Luther King Jr.'s life became an enduring symbol of hope and inspiration for future generations. He grew up witnessing the harsh realities of racial injustice and discrimination; however, his purpose in life began to crystallize as he experienced the transformative power of love and unity through his faith's teachings and his family's support. Inspired by Mahatma Gandhi's philosophy of nonviolent resistance, Dr. King became a charismatic leader in the civil rights movement. His purpose was clear: to lead a crusade against racial injustice and pave the way for a future where people of all races would coexist harmoniously.

In Part 1, you got a handle on recognizing your talents and passions. In Part 2, you learned how to prepare for success and develop a solid personal development plan. So far, you have done a lot of heavy lifting and made many decisions; now, you should have a better view of the life you want to live that will give you joy and happiness. You have a better sense of how to get there, so let us shift our attention to the details of that purpose-driven lifestyle.

Living a life of passion and purpose means having a clear and meaningful direction for your life. Knowing what you value, what principles you live by, and how you want to contribute to your community is essential because a purpose-driven life can bring you many benefits.

Why All the Focus on a Purpose-Driven Life?

Happiness is what most people desire, even above getting rich. Of course, we want to get rich, but changes in the 21st century have redefined how wealth is obtained when people realized that even rich people may not be happy. The events of 9/11 and the COVID-19 pandemic made people refocus on being happy instead of winning the "rat race" to wealth. Happiness and joy come from having a strong sense of purpose, and living your passion is the best way to live this purpose and do what you enjoy.

Living your passion and purpose will improve your physical and mental health. When you go to the doctor, they always ask if you have a strong "family or friends" network. The reason they ask is quite simple. Scientific studies have proven that a strong support network can reduce your chances of depression, anxiety, and loneliness. Other studies have shown that marriage can add 10 years to a person's life. Whether you want to be married or not, your relationships depend on you knowing what you like and dislike. A life based on your passion is the best way to communicate who you are and what you want from life to your family, friends, and partner.

Let's go back to money for a moment. Doing the work in Part 1 and Part 2 of this book can help you achieve your career and financial goals, and achieving these goals can enable you to invest in 401K and Roth IRA wealth-building accounts. It can motivate you to work harder while experiencing more joy and performing better at your job. Mapping skills to jobs can help you pick a company that respects employees while paying a great wage. And, some of them will even let you work from home. As I said earlier, some of you are focusing on happiness and joy instead of getting wealthy.

Too many people waste time and money trying to figure out how to be happy and joyful but come up short. When you have passion and purpose, you can focus your energy and money on what matters most to you. Because you are planning this out early in life, you can prioritize your goals, set realistic deadlines, and overcome issues that get in the way. Newer generations are challenging many big questions in life—questions like "Should I go to college?", "Should I follow in my parent's footsteps?", "Should I get married?", and "Should I become a parent?"

Those questions are too big for one book, but the point is that new ideas, methods, approaches, and solutions are needed for the next generation to answer those questions correctly. Getting answers to these questions is life's next big mystery, and I know this book can help you sort those out.

As you can see, living a purpose-driven lifestyle can enrich your life in many ways. It can help you find meaning, fulfillment, and joy in everything you do. In addition, sharing that purpose with someone you love will help you appreciate why you do it and help them get joy of their own. Your loved ones can also help you stay on track and encourage you when things are not going well. The last point is that you will have no regrets about how you lived your life and the difference you made.

In the following four chapters of Part 3, we will cover the following topics:

- ✓ Developing a lifestyle model to achieve balance in life
- ✓ Developing your goals, mini-goals, and milestones
- ✓ Understanding the importance of close friends and cultivating five great ones
- ✓ Understanding the economic cycles for making money and valuing the need to learn new skills continuously

Chapter 11 – Develop a Lifestyle Model

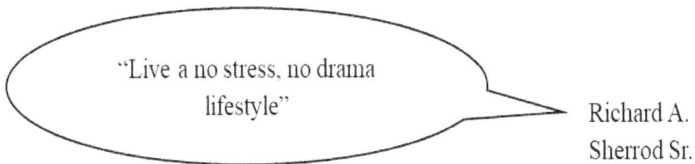

"Live a no stress, no drama lifestyle"

Richard A. Sherrod Sr.

In this chapter, I want to start by sharing a model I created 30 years ago to help me get more balance in life. I was serious about my work life but quickly realized my success was at the expense of my family, friends, neighbors, and wife. Creating this model allowed me to clarify my time, which is set at 24 hours per day for everyone. The model is called Principles for Living, Four Cornerstones of Life.

Before we go on, let's look at the importance of understanding our values and principles as we define our lifestyle. Doing so is essential for a fulfilling life because knowing your core values allows you to align your goals and actions accordingly. This alignment makes pursuing happiness and purpose more meaningful because it resonates with what truly matters to you. Values also serve as a compass during decision-making, guiding you toward choices that align with your beliefs. When faced with challenges, knowing your principles helps build resilience, allowing you to navigate adversity more effectively.

Living in alignment with your values fosters authenticity, attracting meaningful relationships and experiences. Additionally, reflecting on your values leads to self-discovery, helping you understand who you are, what motivates you, and what brings you joy. Understanding values and principles empowers you to live a purpose-driven life, fostering happiness and fulfillment.

Question: What principles do you use to guide your life?

Now, let's return to the model for achieving balance in life.

What Does Work and Family Balance Mean?

Everyone speaks about work-life balance, but few people take action to ensure a balance. Experts say that having balance in life makes employees better at doing work. Few employees can focus on troubleshooting problems at work while thinking about issues with family and close friends. Therefore, if we spend more conscious time on balance, we can perform better and be creative at work.

Balancing work and family also reduces stress, promotes better mental health, and lowers the risk of burnout. Not spending most of your time thinking about work enables you to think about improving your family relationships, including communication, trust, and emotional connection, which lead to healthier relationships.

Why Focus on Commitment to Family and Friends?

Most people say family and friends are a priority to them. They always say they should have called their brother or visited their mother more often. The reality is that most people spend less than 20% of their time thinking about and planning time around family and friends. The proof is this: If the third person that comes to your mind were to disappear, would you say that you spent a great deal of time with them? Most people would say no and regret, "I wish I had called them or visited them instead of letting months go by."

You should spend 40% of your time thinking and planning for family and friends. By doing this, you will gain a level of peace that you never thought was possible.

Doctors insist that we live longer if we have a supportive circle of family and friends. This factor is included in health assessments, and you might pay more for insurance if you lack a strong support network. Meaningful relationships with family and friends contribute to our happiness and overall health.

Why Focus on Self-Fulfillment?

You might assume that prioritizing yourself would naturally take up most of your free time. The sad reality is that most people spend the least amount of time thinking about what makes them happy and sacrifice themselves first to do everything else. You cannot respect others until you respect yourself, and you cannot love others until you learn how to love yourself. This might sound hokey, but when was the last time you did something just for yourself because you thought it was important and planned it ahead of time? We simply need to squeeze in a little time to have fun for ourselves.

Now, you must develop a roadmap for yourself. What do you believe is essential? Who do you value most? Where and how do you want your years to pass? What hobbies do you have for fun? How do you relax? What would you die for? What anchors do you have in life, such as church, charity work, or being a great parent? These points and more are critical to your understanding of yourself. Once you fully understand yourself, you can spend most of your time thinking about family, friends, and your community. You will not obsess much about work because you will understand that work is a necessary means to an end of peace and happiness.

We should spend at least 30% of our time thinking about ourselves and what makes us happy. Others have a view of you, so part of being true to yourself is being good in your behavior and deeds. To be good, you have to do good.

Why Focus on Empathy for Others in Your Community?

Humans are communal by nature. We cannot be isolated for an extended period and need to connect with others outside our family. When we move into a community, we are often busy living life and do not take the time to get to know the neighbors. We may not have gatherings like barbeques and block parties. Science suggests that humans will become insane if isolated for too long, so the mental effect of a lack of community is real and proven by science.

Most people often complain that they want to spend more time getting to know their neighbors and volunteering to help others in the community. You may have New Year's resolutions that involve committing to charity work and participating in local neighborhood programs to help children. We all know that New Year's resolutions fall by the wayside, and sadly, most people do not know their neighbor next to them within three homes away. A village cannot raise a child today because most neighbors do not know each other's names.

We should spend 25% of our thoughts on our community efforts, which include charity work helping others.

The Need to Work Is Self-Evident, Pay the Bills.

Work is not last because it is not as important. We know that work is vital to life's pursuits and happiness as defined by industrialized societies. Work also provides essential friendships and relationships that are supportive and fulfilling. However, work rules and processes dictate where you show up, what you do, and how you do it. Therefore, perfecting process compliance becomes the discussion in most staff meetings. We have degrees and decades of experience, so complying does not take much thinking.

You only need to spend 5% of your time thinking about work because the boss spends 95% of their time telling you what to do. This does not include preparing for work, such as college, projects, or looking for work.

More thinking time is required if you want to be creative and innovative, but many company rules do not allow flexibility. A healthy person with a support group and a feeling of achievement will always do better work.

You Must Change Your Behavior

Before you change your life based on a purpose, you need to understand what behaviors need to change. In Figure 6 below, we guide you through several questions identifying helpful and harmful behaviors.

Figure 6

Behavior Change
Planning Model

What behaviors are <u>helpful</u> for your future that you <u>are</u> doing and should <u>continue</u> doing?	What behaviors are <u>helpful</u> for your future that <u>you are not</u> currently doing but should <u>start</u> doing?
Enter your response These behaviors are good and need to continue	Enter your response These behaviors are good, but I am not doing them now
What behaviors are <u>not helpful</u> for your future that you <u>are</u> doing now but must <u>stop</u> doing?	What behavior is <u>not helpful</u> for your future that you <u>are not</u> doing now and must ensure you <u>never</u> do?
Enter your response These behaviors are bad. I keep doing them but must stop	Enter your response These behaviors are bad, and I don't ever want to do them

The first question in the Behavior Change Planning Model is, "What behaviors are **helpful** for your future that you are doing and should continue doing?" These behaviors are good and need to continue.

The second question is, "What behaviors are **helpful** for your future that you are not currently doing but should start doing?" These behaviors are good, but you are not doing them now. This may require you to learn new skills, so do not forget to add new ones to your development plan.

The third question is, "What behaviors are **not helpful** for your future that you are doing now but must stop doing?" Even though these behaviors are destructive and could get you in trouble, you keep doing them. Some of these are requested or required by others, but you know they are not helping you achieve your goals. You may be doing them because you want to be perceived as supportive. If that is the case, the behavior may foster a good relationship, so consider this before you stop.

The last question is, "What behavior is **not helpful** for your future that you are not doing now and must ensure you never do?" These behaviors are destructive, and you never want to do them because they could derail your future success. Sometimes, people may pick up behaviors they think are desired by hiring managers. But why are you worried about those folks if your "skills to mapping model" excluded specific jobs?

Now, you might be thinking that the exercise above was pretty easy. If you believe that, you were not honest with yourself or your mentor. You must reflect on the truth and admit what you do, even if no one else knows. This exercise is for you, but you cannot gain from it if you do not open up and come clean. So, you must put yourself out of your comfort zone and answer truthfully. If you do not want to do this exercise with a parent, do it with a close friend—they know when you are holding back.

Implementing these changes will be the hard part. According to science, changing a habit can be challenging. Habits are behaviors you do without much thought or effort, and they are associated with your daily routine, friends, and need to fit in at school or work. To change a habit, you need to identify the benefits of it, why it is important to you, and how it fits with your long-term goals. Changing your habits takes time, patience, and lots of willpower.

It is normal to fall short of your new expectations, but keep at it. Do not be too hard on yourself, and reward yourself when you do well. Do not forget that we all make mistakes and that progress is better than perfection.

Key Takeaways

Once you have a daily way of thinking about the Four Cornerstones of Life, what you do and how you use your time changes. You do not sweat the little things because they distract you from what is important. You also do not fight with loved ones because you value them more than anyone else. You do not harm your body because you respect yourself more than alcohol, tattoos, and the latest fads.

Because most of our family and friends accept us as we are, you understand that good practice in life makes progress, and you accept that you are not perfect. Admittedly, this 25-year model may be getting outdated, but it gives you a guide for creating your own high-level living model. Family, friends, community, and self are critical life elements that need to be balanced so we have no regrets later in life.

If you insist on spending 70% of your time thinking about work, make sure your passion is what brings in the income.

Your Next Steps

Develop your life-balance model based on these four cornerstones. Your dedicated thinking times may change depending on your priorities for spending time with family or friends. Ultimately, your passion should drive your purpose and how you make your income. Complete the "Behavior Change Planning Model" indicated in Figure 6 at the back of this book.

In the next chapter, you will learn to set goals, mini-goals, and milestones to ensure success.

Chapter 12 – Develop Your Goals

"Without goals, and plans to reach them, you are like a ship that has set sail with no destination."

Fitzhugh
Dodson

In this chapter, we will build off the previous chapters by taking all your decisions and determining what you will do with them in the short and long term. But first, let us look at why goals are important and how you develop them. Michael Jordan, the basketball legend, exemplified goal setting and planning, and his unwavering focus on winning NBA championships drove him to meticulously train, visualize success, and execute flawlessly on the court. His six NBA titles with the Chicago Bulls are a testament to his commitment to setting goals and developing a plan to achieve them.

A goal is an outcome of the future or result that a person desires, plans, and works to achieve. People have expectations of reaching goals within a specific time by setting deadlines. When a goal is clear in your mind, you clearly understand the tasks needed to achieve that outcome and know what you need to do and how to do it. As you achieve success along the way, the process becomes a source of motivation.

Question: What example comes to mind where you gave up on something because you didn't track whether it was working or not?

There are short-term and long-term goals, so we will cover the difference before we go deeper into this chapter. Short-term goals are objectives you aim to achieve within a relatively brief timeframe, typically weeks to a few months. They focus on immediate actions and outcomes. For example, you may want to complete a project by the end of the week or learn a new skill this month. Long-term goals, on the other hand, extend over a longer duration, often years or even a lifetime. They represent significant achievements or aspirations. Examples include earning a degree, building a successful career, or maintaining a healthy lifestyle throughout your life.

Some factors help you achieve your goals, and others prevent you from reaching them. Some of the key obstacles are a lack of charity, a lack of motivation, a lack of resources, and not correctly allocating time. You can take steps to increase your success at reaching your goals. To start, it would help if you clarified your vision of the future you would like to see. If you achieve what you want in three years, what would your world look like at that time? Feel free to document what you see in your vision so you can share it with your family and mentors.

Next, you must prioritize your time and resources and allocate them effectively. Some people fail because they do not measure their progress or evaluate their results. This task can easily be managed using a tracking form in Microsoft Word, and we will cover how to do this later. Staying motivated is a big one because life happens and other issues will move to the top of your calendar. You can help by reviewing your progress with your mentors and parents to get their motivational pep talks.

One thing most people overlook is the need to learn something new to achieve their goals. You didn't think you had every skill needed to achieve your goal, did you? Learning is a crucial part of the plan, and many goal-setting programs forget to include this vital element. The last thing to mention is celebrating every little win along the way. This pumps up your motivation but also confirms your plan is on track.

Recent models have incorporated steps to minimize these obstacles and have proved effective at helping you get a better outcome. The model we will focus on is called the SMART goal model.

SMART Goals

SMART goals are **S**pecific, **M**easurable, **A**chievable, **R**elevant, and **T**ime-Bound. This model helps you develop clear and actionable goals that are aligned with your future world vision, which can be achieved within a desired timeframe.

So, let's break down each element.

Specific: The goal should be well-defined and clear, answering the questions of what, why, and how.

Measurable: The goal should be quantifiable and have a way to track progress and measure your success. You want to use milestones or weekly measurements to ensure you are progressing toward completing your mini-goals. Each mini-goal leads to a bigger goal.

Achievable: Given the available resources and constraints, the goal should be realistic and attainable. However, stretch goals that push you past your comfort zone are helpful. Goals that are easy to obtain are void of value. At the same time, goals that are impossible to achieve will be frustrating and lead to failure. Your mentors or parents can help with resources and help remove constraints.

Relevant: The goal should be meaningful and aligned with your values, vision, and priorities. Most importantly, it should connect back to your passion and purpose-driving lifestyle.

Time-Bound: The goal should have a deadline or a timeframe, which creates a sense of urgency and helps to prioritize tasks. You do not need to waste time on goals beyond three years because the world will change. You can write them down, but don't plan the details just yet. You must accept that reevaluating and changing your goals is part of life, and you cannot control the rate of change in the world.

Setting SMART goals can increase your chances of success and avoid common pitfalls. SMART goals help people focus their attention, energy, and resources on what matters most and progress toward their desired outcomes.

Mini-Goals

There is an old saying, "How do you eat an elephant? One bite at a time." You could never imagine eating a whole elephant because it is too large. But you can imagine eating a bite, two, or 10 from that elephant. If you take a bite every week, you will eat the elephant at some point. Mini-goals are so important because they help you focus on what you can do, not what you can't do. Tiger Woods wanted to win the Masters golf championship as a young golfer. That was his main goal. However, he probably said, "I just want to win this tournament this week." One bite of the elephant at a time.

Mini-goals are small, specific, and achievable goals that you set for yourself to accomplish in a short period of time. They are designed to help you break down your larger goals into manageable and actionable steps and to build progress and confidence along the way.

Mini-goals are different from main goals in several ways. They are smaller and more focused, while main goals tend to be broader and more visionary. Mini-goals are usually accomplished within a few days, weeks, or months, whereas main goals may take three years or more to achieve. Specific tasks or skills are often related to mini-goals, while larger outcomes or lifestyles are related to main goals. Mini-goals are usually prioritized lower than main goals, which are considered more important and strategic. In addition, mini-goals are designed to provide quick wins and boost motivation, whereas main goals require sustained effort and perseverance. Finally, main goals test your willpower, whereas mini-goals kick your willpower to the side.

Mini-goals can be an effective way to achieve main goals, as they help you focus your attention, energy, and resources on what is essential and practical in the short term. Life gets in the way of main goals, but you can do a mini-goal this week. Let's say your main goal is to improve your net worth by $100,000 in three years. You could set mini-goals of $25,000 within 12 months. This seems more realistic and achievable. It would help if you had milestones to set your path on how to get the $25,000.

Milestones

Milestones are short-term, actionable steps that achieve a mini-goal or primary goal. If you need to get $25,000 within 12 months, your milestones might be opening an investment account next week, getting your parents to seed the account with starting funds within two weeks, and building your credit score to 700 within 30 days. These might seem unrelated to getting $25,000, but look closer. Each milestone tells you if you are on track to get the result. If your credit does not improve, your parents may not want to invest the seed money. If they do not invest the seed money, your account sits empty and cannot grow during a hot market, providing a 27% return on investment. Each milestone you complete indicates that your bigger plan is working and likely producing a more significant result.

Key Takeaways

In this chapter, we covered goals and why you must have them to live a purpose-driven lifestyle fueled by passion. We defined the SMART goal model and helped you understand each element of the model. We also explained the difference between goals, mini-goals, and milestones so you clearly understand how to use each. Capture your decisions on the goal-tracking form in Figure 7 below.

Figure 7

My Goals

	Description of goal	Why do I want this goal and what is the desired outcome?	When will I achieve it?	What happens if this goal is not met?	How will I measure this goal?	What are my weekly milestones of achievement?	Status?
Main Goal #1 =							
mini goal #1 =							
mini goal #2 =							
mini goal #3 =							
Main Goal #2 =							
mini goal #1 =							
mini goal #2 =							
mini goal #3 =							
Main Goal #3 =							
mini goal #1 =							
mini goal #2 =							
mini goal #3 =							

Consider these things as you link your goals to your talents and passions, and think about the passion that will fuel your future. Happiness is best achieved by enthusiastically using your talents, which makes you smile just thinking about them. Be clear and precise about how you will use your talents and skills to pay the bills. What do you want to do in 5, 10, 15 and 20 years? Look further than you can see over the horizon, think big, and remember that achieving three-year goals at the highest level is possible with skills training and a network of supporters.

Do not forget to set milestones for every week and every month so you know if you are on track or need to adjust your training and experience. Next, decide what is essential and what you will sacrifice because being disciplined to achieve your goals means you cannot chase every fad or dare from your friends. Do not do what everyone is doing—instead, your passion should fuel your focus. Update your development and implementation plan every three months because stuff happens in life. Adjust as you go, but stay focused on where you are going.

Your Next Steps

Your actions should be clear by now, and you should write down your goals. To do that, meet with your mentors, parents, and friends to discuss your future vision of life and ask for their input on how you should get there. After a robust and challenging discussion, write down your three-year goals. We include a form at the back of this book so you can capture your goals, due dates, and other key information. Do not forget that your personal development plan must be updated based on these new goals and skills you need to learn to enable your success.

Chapter 13 – Cultivate Five Great Friends

"A real friend is one who walks in when the rest of the world walks out."

Walter Winchell

In this chapter, we will take you out of your comfort zone with a discussion about friendships, their value, and the purpose they serve. Great friendships are an essential part of living a healthy life, and basically, friendships are special bonds between people with common interests, values, and passions. Having great friendships is vital for several reasons. Friends provide a sense of belonging and purpose, and they can help you celebrate good times and provide support during bad times. They can also help you cope with sadness, anxiety, and despair. Friends can boost your joy and reduce your stress, while encouraging you to pursue your passions and dreams and motivating you to work hard. Importantly, friendships can help prevent isolation, loneliness, and depression. Teenagers and young adults with strong social connections have a reduced risk of many significant health problems, including depression, high blood pressure, and experimental drug use.

Question: How many close friends do you have, and how long have you known them?

Friendship Research

According to a 2004 Gallup poll, Americans have an average of eight to nine close friends (Carroll 2004). That being said, research suggests that having a few close friends is more important than having many acquaintances. This poll shows 55% have five or fewer close friends, with 2% having no close friends at all.

A recent survey found the average Facebook user has 155 friends on the platform but only considers 43 contacts to be genuine friends. More shockingly, they would only trust four of their Facebook friends in a crisis.

According to a recent study, adults with four or five friends enjoy the highest levels of life satisfaction (Degges-White 2019).

Types of Friendships

Acquaintances are the people we see on a regular basis that we "kind of know." We know them at least well enough to make idle small talk, but we do not have the emotional attachment needed to deepen the connection.

Casual friends are typically those with whom you spend time within shared activities or with whom you cross paths regularly and have gotten to know enough to feel ready to call a "friend." You might like all the members of your math class, laugh with them during the meetings, and even hang out with them outside of class, but they are people that you probably would not hang out with if you did not share this particular class.

Close friends usually start as acquaintances who turn into casual friends. With mutual respect and affinity, you begin to share a little more about yourself, and they do the same. This mutual sharing deepens the relationship, and you continue to enjoy getting to know one another and spending time together. Close friends are the ones that you call when life sucks so bad that you want to scream or hide. They are those you trust with many of your secrets and those who put up with you even when you are in a lousy mood or need to talk at 2 am. Close friends are the ones who share your passion, dreams, and hopes for the future.

Intimate friends are the most intensely connected. These are the friends you let into the inner world of your heart and mind, who you trust with your deepest secrets, and who you know will never let you down or betray your trust.

You will always have acquaintances and casual friends, but do not confuse them with close or intimate friends. Your close friends are the ones you need in your success plan and on your team. Some of your Facebook, Instagram, TikTok, and X (formerly Twitter) friends may be the secret bullies spreading negative information about you—you do not need life-changing input from them.

Key Takeaways

Hopefully, you were not out of your comfort zone for too long. You should have a clear view of the different types of friends you have and why each type is important in your life. You should now see the value of focusing more on your close friends, as they will stick with you when you need them the most. The friendship research should have caught your attention. You already know that if you call all your friends to show up at your house tomorrow, only a few will show up.

Your Next Steps

Consider your friend list and decide who your close or intimate friends are. Narrow your list down to the top five you desire to be your lifelong advisors. Call them and discuss what you need from them and confirm they want to fulfill that role. Next, run the list by your parents because they may know things you do not know, and be open to their input even if you dislike what they say about your friends. Remember, in Chapter 7, you developed your success team of five mentors. These are experts in their field and are adults with experience that can help you grow.

The five close friends in this chapter are the ones who will inspire you to fulfill your dreams and push you to live your passion. They may share your passion, can plan their lives along your journey, and genuinely want to go on the ride with you and develop a life together.

In the next chapter, you will get a different perspective on why continuous learning is essential. We referred to continuous learning a few times earlier in this book and want to give you a value-based reason to adopt this philosophy. We will do that by discussing why children cannot make money the way their parents did not that long ago, and we will show you how to approach it differently so you can stay ahead of the game.

Chapter 14 – Live a Life of Continuous Learning

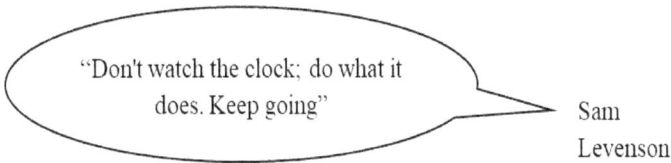

"Don't watch the clock; do what it does. Keep going"

Sam
Levenson

There are many ways to start this chapter about continuous learning. Recognizing that many of you do not like learning as a principle, I need to make this point in a way that will take you out of your comfort zone. You see, learning is not just about gaining knowledge but about staying ahead of changing economic trends. Look around—many of you are struggling to find ways to make money and to survive in the 21st century.

The reason for that is twofold. You have not identified your passions and currently make money doing things you dislike. Second, you are trying to find success based on what worked for your parents. Without a passion, you will not do what you love and be happy each week. You feel the anxiety and despair setting in but do not know what to do about it.

Your parents cannot tell you how the economic cycles have changed, but you cannot make money the way they did. Although this may seem daunting, there is hope for figuring this out. For me to break this down in a way you can understand and visualize, I need to go back 2,000 years.

Question: What changes in the past five years make you uncomfortable and unsure of the future?

In this chapter, we will explore the economic life cycles of money and how everyday people succeed financially. Trust me, we will connect this all back to continuous learning, and you will get it in the end.

Periods of Economic Change

Succeed with Your Hands

There have been several economic cycles over the past 2,000 or so. We will use the United States calendar starting in the year 0 through 2023. The first period to understand is the Agrarian economy or agriculture; in this cycle, people succeeded based on the land they owned and worked to produce food and other items. Peasants who did not own land worked for those who did or were enslaved people who worked the fields. This period covered the years before the year 0 to about 1650. The life expectancy in 1600 was around 43 years.

Therefore, families had around 37 generations to pass down skills needed to make a living. A farmer or sheep herder could pass down skills to their children, grandchildren, and great-grandchildren. Children born during this time did not worry about how to survive; they simply did what their parents did and were successful. Manorialism was the economic system that governed agricultural production and land use and controlled all aspects of the agriculture business ("Manorialism Summary" n.d.).

Succeed by Taking and Trading Goods

The years from about 1650 to about 1850 were a period of exploration and discovery. European powers established colonies and other lands and engaged in mercantile practice and exchange. The extraction of resources from colonies fueled economic growth in Europe during this time, giving many a chance to make money beyond agriculture. The life expectancy in 1860 was about 39 years old, so this 200-year period covered about five generations. Again, that meant fathers could teach their children and grandchildren how to succeed and make money in the same way as the parents.

You can see that those 1650 years before sustained about 37 generations, but this 200-year period only sustained about five generations of children. Together, the first two periods covered about 1,850 years when children did not worry about how to make money.

Succeed with Technology

Then came the Industrial Revolution from about 1850 to about 1940. This 90-year period marked a significant shift from agricultural economies to industrialization. Innovations in machines, steam power, and transportation led to increased manufacturing and urbanization, and innovators built factories to mass-produce cars, food, clothing, and other essential items. Many had to learn new skills to work in these factories. Many parents were lost as they could no longer teach their children how to make money, so children left home for the big cities, where communities were built to keep workers near factories.

The life expectancy in 1920, before the Great Depression, was 54 years old. That meant this 90-year period could only sustain about 1.7 generations. That meant the kids could start off during what their parents did but had to learn new skills before they had children of their own.

Succeed by Selling Worldwide and Using Your Brain

Expanded travel and technology meant people could make money by selling, trading, and exchanging goods worldwide. Imperialism and global trade dominated the late 19th and 20th centuries. This period saw the rise of multinational corporations and the spread of capitalism worldwide.

World wars disrupted global economies, but post-war recovery led to unprecedented economic growth through 1990, particularly in the United

States. The middle class was booming, supported by the United States government's new programs.

The late 20th century saw the rise of activist governmental economic policies characterized by deregulation, privatization, and increased globalization. This period witnessed the rapid growth of financial markets and the creation of multinational corporations. It seemed overnight that you could make money using other people's money on Wall Street. Baby boomers could invest in 401k accounts and become millionaires in ways their parents could never imagine.

Succeed in Information Collection and Sharing

The information age and technological revolution in the late 1900s and early 2000s meant parents and children alike were struggling to keep up with how to make money. The PC, iPhone, and other information devices meant people were willing to pay to get information quickly. Newspapers and magazines had to shift to digital outputs, and students were learning remotely from their homes. The emergence of the internet and digital technologies in the late 20th century revolutionized industries, leading to the emergence of tech giants like Microsoft, Apple, IBM, and Google.

This new knowledge-based economy meant you could no longer survive with your hands; you had to use your brain. This period is shifting fast, and students and parents alike are finding it hard to keep up. Even if you graduated with a degree in 2023, your skills may be obsolete before you can get a job, thanks to AI and advanced learning machines.

Succeed by Using Machines

Let us wrap this up by looking at the pace of change in the past five years. AI emerged to take on whole industries like finance, law, medicine, and computer science. Many say one way to be successful in the 21st century is to learn how to use AI to help you do your job better. The point is not to scare you but to point out in this chapter that economic cycles are a normal part of the world economy, and the pace of change is increasing.

Parents can no longer teach their children how to succeed based on what the parents did, and children are struggling to find a path forward. AI and advanced robotics will not replace all jobs, but they will change the type of jobs available. You must be open to change and continuously learning as a way of staying ahead of the game.

Whether you like it or not, the game changes, so develop your action plan and start early. As the saying goes, "The early bird catches the worm." That means you must adapt quickly and change your mindset from resistance to learning.

An Alternative Approach

Younger generations are struggling to find passion in private-sector jobs. It seems private-sector companies are reducing labor costs, increasing pressure on productivity, and laying people off more frequently. Mandates to return to the office, unstructured work processes, and massive layoffs have caused anxiety, despair, and uncertainty for millions of young adults. Many young adults in Generation Z, in particular, don't see hope in the American Dream. They believe the American Dream their parents enjoy is not realistic for them. Therefore, they must create their version of the American Dream based on 21st century realities.

An alternative to the private-sector job market is the public sector. That means working for the government or the education system. There are three big reasons to consider working for public sector organizations. First, job security is generally better. Public sector jobs are linked to their budget, and government spending does not significantly decrease year after year. Government and school system departments are rarely eliminated outright. They may not replace those leaving or push for early retirement programs, but layoffs are not the norm in the public sector.

Second, the public sector benefits are usually better than those of the private sector. Health insurance at low out-of-pocket cost, retirement plans such as pensions, and other benefits make the public sector a great choice to reduce anxiety about caring for a family. Most private-sector jobs no longer offer a guaranteed pension, and you have to save for retirement using a 401K plan. Government jobs often provide consistent working hours, and you know what the job entails. Private-sector jobs rarely have 9-to-5 working hours, and bosses require employees to work late, often without overtime pay.

Government jobs never require an employee to stay late without paying overtime. Annual time off is typically better in the first five years of employment. The public sector's pay scales are structured around job types and titles. On the other hand, in the private sector, a new hire can make more money than a 10-year employee, and employees often complain about differing pay within the same job. In addition, by working in the public sector, your student loan debt can be forgiven after ten years.

Key Takeaways

In this chapter, we reviewed the different significant shifts in economic cycles. We went from agriculture, which had sustained more than 35 generations, to 21st century skills, which became obsolete within a few years. That brings me back to why you must continuously learn new skills because you do not have a choice. The biggest takeaway from this chapter is to recognize what economic cycle you live in, which is not the same as your parents'.

Your parents cannot transfer skills to you because their economic cycle has come to an end. Children must look forward to understanding how money is made and how passions can fuel a successful life. That is why we developed a "success team" in Chapter 7, with experts who can help you see future changes and provide the learning advice needed to be on the cutting edge of change.

Although I took you out of your comfort zone, I hope you can see that the pace of change will dictate your need to learn new skills. Change is constant, so prepare for a continual adaptation and learning life. Being uncomfortable with how money is made is far better than being depressed. The reason is that depression sometimes blocks you from seeing a solution, while being uncomfortable pushes you to find readily available answers. This book is a significant first step to developing your own American Dream.

And remember that working for the government or school system is an excellent alternative to the "hustle society." This may not be a great option for everyone, but many will find the benefits too good to ignore.

Your Next Steps

You need to study and research how money is made in the 21st century. Do not be afraid to discuss this with your parents, using the idea of challenging old norms and methods. Once you know how money can be made, adjust your talents, passion, and skills assessment before implementing your learning development plan.

In Part 4, you will learn how to build a great credit score and be challenged to rethink your relationship with money.

Part 4

Change Your Relationship with Money

PART 4 | Change Your Relationship with Money

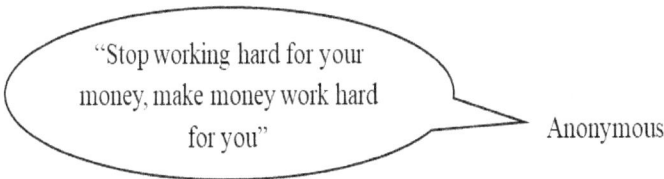

"Stop working hard for your money, make money work hard for you"   Anonymous

That last chapter was a doozy, wasn't it? Hopefully, you learned that for the average person, making money is predicated on knowing your economic cycle. In 2019, there were 12 million "401K millionaire households" in the US. These millionaires did not get there just by using their hands and skills but by using new methods to grow wealth. Mississippi is one of the poorest states but still has 47,279 millionaires. Millennial millionaires own an average of three properties, and generations in the 20th century found real estate the best way to grow wealth.

Only 20% of Americans inherit their riches, and the other 80% are self-made, first-generation millionaires. Things changed a lot in the 21st century regarding housing, inflation, and daily living expenses, and Gen Z took notice and decided to live a more modest lifestyle. Gone are the expensive cars and big homes because they know the world is changing and that they need to treat money differently than their free-spending parents.

As mentioned in Chapter 14, working for the government or school system may eliminate your student loan debt after a few years of work.

This alone could offset a smaller paycheck and enable you to live a better life financially.

Let me tell you a quick story about Olivia, a tech millionaire swimming in wealth and surrounded by the glow of her luxurious lifestyle. Private jets, penthouse suites, and the latest gadgets filled her days, but Olivia felt an unsettling emptiness beneath the reality of wealth. The constant flow of notifications couldn't drown out the silence of her discontent. In a world connected by technology, Olivia was disconnected from true happiness. One day, confronted by the cold connection of her smart home, she decided to break free from the digital chains.

Trading virtual relationships for genuine smiles, Olivia ventured into the analog world. Simple joys like coffee with a friend and unplugged sunsets became her new currency. In embracing the authenticity of human connection, Olivia discovered a wealth more profound than all her high-tech toys. She found the richness of a fulfilled and happy heart.

In Part 4, we will cover your relationship with money and how you can change that so that money works hard for you while you enjoy life. Generations of children seem to fall into the same money traps: bad credit scores, lack of financial literacy, lack of saving and retirement planning, and living paycheck-to-paycheck are issues that repeat from one generation to the next. We will cover the fundamentals of money and explain how to build a great credit score, break the cycle of poverty using "compound interest," and reexamine the effectiveness of starting a business while you are young.

Chapter 15 – Master the Credit Score

"A bad credit score is like a door slamming shut on whatever you want to do in life."

Chris
Brogan

In this chapter, we will cover FICA credit scores and how to build a great score. A credit score is a three-digit number representing the amount of risk a borrower poses to a lender. It is managed by the big credit bureaus, which issue monetary credit for people looking to buy goods and services without cash.

Scores ranging from 300 to 850 help lenders evaluate a borrower's creditworthiness at a glance. The higher the score, the better the creditworthiness of the borrower. A score of 670 or above is generally considered good, while a score below 580 is considered poor. The big three credit bureaus are Equifax, Experian, and TransUnion. An excellent credit score is not just for buying goods but is necessary when applying for an apartment.

Question: How many categories make up your credit score? How has a bad score affected your life in the past?

You may not realize how important a strong credit score is in America. Hiring managers often pull your credit score before offering you a job.

Landlords will always pull your credit before deciding on your apartment application. Some high-level memberships may pull your credit before accepting your membership, and many have complained that golf, tennis, and other clubs exclude people with low credit scores. It may not seem right, but more groups are pulling your credit score.

US law enables you to have access to your credit report annually from the big three credit bureaus. Reviewing these reports is vital to catching mistakes and issues that may negatively impact your credit score.

Credit Categories

Five categories make up a credit score. First, the amounts you owe represent 30% of your total credit score. The idea is to keep your utilization of total credit low. If you are using a lot of your available credit, this may indicate that you are overextended. Banks can interpret this to mean you are at a higher risk of defaulting on your credit lines.

The second category is payment history, which represents 35% of your total score. The first thing any lender wants to know is whether you have paid past credit accounts on time. This category helps a lender determine the risk it will take when extending credit, and it is the most important factor in a FICO Score.

The third category is the length of credit history, which represents 15% of your total score. Lenders look at how long your credit accounts have been established, including the age of your oldest account, the age of your newest account, and the average age of all your accounts.

The fourth category is how much new credit you have, representing 10% of your total score. Research shows that opening several credit accounts in a short time represents a greater risk, especially for people who do not have a long credit history. If you can avoid it, try not to open too many accounts too quickly.

The last category is your credit mix, representing 10% of your total score. FICO Scores will consider your mix of credit cards, retail accounts, recurring loans, installment accounts, car loans, mortgage loans, and other types of loans.

How to Build Great Credit

Many online websites are designed to help you build a great credit score. If you search for websites or YouTube videos, you will find plenty of them. You can use some traditional ways to boost your credit score, like applying for a secured credit card. A secured card can be easier to get than a traditional unsecured credit card because it requires a cash deposit as collateral in case you default on payments. The deposit you will need to make depends on the credit card, which typically equals the credit limit.

You can use a credit-building website like Chime.com. With Chime, you won't pay any annual fees or interest on your Credit Builder card. This makes it a cost-effective option for credit building. Applying for the Chime Credit Builder doesn't require a credit check, making it accessible even if you have limited or no credit history. Chime encourages responsible credit use—you can instantly lock your card to prevent fraud and build credit using your own money, minimizing the risk of debt and missed payments. Chime reports your on-time payments to Equifax, Experian, and TransUnion.

This helps increase your credit score over time. Chime's "SpotMe" feature provides fee-free coverage for transactions up to $200, adding an extra layer of security while building credit. Remember that other credit-building options like Chime can help you build or improve a great credit score without spending a lot of money.

Another way to build credit is becoming an authorized user. Ask a trusted family member or friend to add you to a credit card as an authorized user. This could be an excellent strategy for parents wanting to help their teenagers get started. Regardless of whether you use the card, it will appear on your credit report and help you build credit—just make sure the card reports authorized users to the credit bureaus.

In addition, you should consider a credit union card. Parents may be members of a specific group with special access to financial services because military members, police, firefighters, and others can have membership in these institutions. The good news is that benefits apply to the family, so teenagers can get access when they otherwise would not qualify. A community credit union is a wise place to start for a quality credit product that reports to the credit bureaus because these financial institutions often understand the community's needs and have a mission to help their customers and families get ahead.

Make sure you receive credit for rent and utility payments. You or your landlord can sign up for a rent reporting service to put your rent payments on your credit report. You can also add points to your credit score with Experian Boost, a free service that gives you credit for timely utility, telecom, and certain streaming service payments.

Also, you can get a store or gas station credit card. These can be easier to qualify for than many unsecured cards, but one caveat is that gas stations and store cards charge higher interest rates than others. So, you should always pay off your balance. The idea is to use them for small amounts to build your credit score. Do not make the mistake of maxing out your credit limit on these high-interest accounts.

Don't Forget about Budgeting

John Maxwell once said, "If you don't tell your money where to go, you will wonder where it went."

There are six reasons you need a budget.

1) It helps you keep your eye on the prize. You can see how to get to your goal.

2) It ensures you do not spend money you do not have, so you stop overspending.

3) It leads to a happier retirement and reduces stress.

4) It prepares you for emergencies and allows you to be flexible.

5) It sheds light on bad spending habits so you can save money. Following a budget will help you get more sleep.

6) Last, you cannot ignore budgeting because it will catch up with you!

There are significant reasons why you must budget before things catch up with you. Costs associated with raising children have been rising fast for at least 20 years. So, if you are a parent, you must budget for these growing costs, including daycare or after-school care. That might prevent some parents from working due to the high price. Even with health insurance, medical expenses can be devastating and lead to bankruptcy if not planned correctly. Because people are living longer, care for the elderly is often overlooked but can cost thousands of dollars per year.

Emergencies will happen but are often not included in the budget, so have a "rainy day" fund for these unplanned events. Most people do not have $1,000 in the bank to cover emergencies, and many cannot get a credit card. That means you may be one flat tire away from missing work and losing a job. I know of several women who lost jobs because their children got sick and they could not afford childcare on those unplanned days. And don't forget those emergencies tied to your apartment or house—there is always something to fix or spend money on inside your home.

Budgeting may be tricky for some, so use a Microsoft template or app to keep track of everything. Figure out your after-tax income and write down your spending by day. Have money automatically deducted from your check so you do not have to think about moving your money into savings. The last big thing under budget planning is retirement savings. Savings should come out first because you cannot stop the future but can prepare for it.

Parents must think carefully about financial literacy for their children. Many nonprofit organizations offer free workshops on managing money and building wealth. For example, the Sherrod Foundation Inc., at sherrodfoundation.org, offers free workshops on building great credit and wealth for high school students.

Let's review some everyday things to do and not do, as indicated in Figure 8 below.

Figure 8

Do's and Don'ts of Managing Good Credit

Do	Don't
❑ Pay your bills on time	❑ Pay for a service you can perform yourself
❑ Pay down debt	❑ Use a credit settlement company
❑ Keep some accounts open even after paid	❑ Spend more than you earn, pay with cash
❑ Take responsibility for your financial health	❑ Allow negative credit to stand in the way of your dreams
❑ Keep you utilization rates at 10% or less	❑ Stay in the "debt trap"
❑ Seek professional help when you don't know what to do	❑ Don't open a lot of credit card accounts, especially from pre-approved mailers
❑ Monitor your credit regularly	

© Copyright 2023 by Tips4Living LLC

You should always put your bill due date on your calendar—that way, you won't forget. Some people think they should close accounts that are paid off, but leaving some long-standing accounts open is essential. Accounts with many years on them will increase your credit, even if you never use them again. You may not know that credit repair companies make billions of dollars doing what you could do for free, so avoid them and get help from free nonprofit organizations.

Key Takeaways

In this chapter, we reviewed what a credit score is and how you can build a great FICA score before graduating high school. We discussed ways parents can help and how building financial literacy is critical. We covered why you should budget your money and how to get started. Our ideas do not cost money, so avoid the credit repair companies.

Your Next Steps

Request a copy of your credit report. You get one free one annually, so request yours every four months. First, get one from Equifax. Then, four months later, get one from Experian. The last one is four months later from TransUnion. By staggering them, you are checking for errors every four months. We covered SMART goals in Chapter 12, so do not forget to set financial goals and update your tracking sheet to include your new goals. Do this update after you finish each chapter in Part 4.

Use a budget template within Microsoft Excel or download an app to complete your budget. Lay out your budget for everything that requires money for the month. Now that you have the budget, track everything you spend for one month. Every penny should be accounted for on this tracking sheet. At the end of the month, compare the month's spending to the month's budget. Now, you can see the problems.

In the next chapter, you will learn the fundamentals of money and the secret to building generational wealth and understand the different types of investment accounts.

Chapter 16 – Learn the Fundamentals of Money

"The goal isn't more money. The goal is living life on your terms."

Will Smith

In this chapter, we will cover the fundamentals of money and show you how to break the cycle of poverty and create generational wealth. But first, let me acknowledge that getting wealthy may not be your goal. You may be on a path to pursuing your passions and living a modest lifestyle, and that is okay. Using the "skills to jobs mapping model," we showed you that several jobs and companies might support your passion and pay you a livable wage. However, there are several fundamentals everyone needs to know about money and wealth.

Question: How would you rate your knowledge of the factors that affect money and wealth on a scale of 1 to 10?

This is a huge topic, and I cannot cover all the elements of managing money and building wealth. I intend to cover the common fundamentals that apply to most people over their lifetime. Do you remember when companies were loyal to their employees and employees worked at the same companies for decades? That loyalty is gone. Companies today will likely lay off employees before their 10th anniversary, so building tenure is unlikely in today's multinational business structure. In addition, younger employees cannot stomach the idea of working for the same company for 30 years, and they are not afraid to move from one job to another.

The current thinking for young adults is to have six income streams to offset the possibility of losing income in a given year. We will cover examples of income streams later in Chapter 18 so you get an idea of how this works and how simple it is to implement. But first, let's look at the fundamentals of money.

First, The Big Secret

Wealthy families have enjoyed money working hard for them for generations, while others have worked hard for their money and are doing a poor job at it. This assessment is derived from the savings rate, retirement savings rates, debt load, and low net worth of middle-class people. So, what is the secret that wealthy families have enjoyed for so long? It is "compound interest." The first thing I want you to learn is what compound interest is and how it works.

Compound interest is a powerful tool to build wealth over time. It is when the interest you earn on a balance in an investment account is reinvested, earning you more interest. A wise man once said, "Money makes money, and the money that money makes makes more money." Compound interest accelerates the growth of your investments over decades. It works by adding the earned interest to your principal balance, which then increases your interest, compounding your returns. The larger your balance gets, the larger those interest amounts become, thanks to math or exponential growth.

In other words, compound interest is a way to make your money work hard for you. It is a simple concept, but it can profoundly impact your finances over your lifetime. By reinvesting your earnings, you can grow wealth faster and achieve your financial goals sooner. And, there is better news: 401K savings account deposits are taken from pre-taxed money.

That means you get a tax break upfront directly related to your tax rate. And, there is better news still: A ROTH IRA savings account is already taxed, so you never pay more taxes after you take retirement deductions (after five years and 59.5 years old).

As indicated earlier, there were 12 million "401K millionaire households" in the US in 2019. In the past, the easiest way for baby boomers to gain millionaire status was to invest in a 401K or ROTH IRA account while working, and it worked like magic. As of the fourth quarter of 2021, baby boomers born between 1946 and 1964 control approximately half of all US household wealth, which amounts to more than $71 trillion (Pino 2022).

Although baby boomers made out well, 34 million Americans were living in poverty, and women made up 56% of those in poverty. Some know the secret, and some do not.

Three Basic Accounts to Have

To be financially independent, you need three types of accounts. First, you need an emergency fund. We covered that earlier, and you get the idea that this fund covers what you cannot anticipate. It would help to have at least six months' worth of spending in this account. It is not just the flat tire that should concern you—what happens if you get laid off or hospitalized?

The second type of account is the basic savings account. You save money to pay for your children's college or that annual vacation, and how about giving Christmas presents to the children and saving to buy a new car? These are short-term saving accounts because you intend to use the money for something specific. It would be best to put these savings into interest-bearing accounts like high-yield CDs that can be withdrawn at any time. You can also use a mutual or stock fund account to get higher returns on your money. These accounts, offered by firms like Charles Schwab, are liquid, so you can take the money out anytime.

The third type of account is the big one, an investment account. I will cover this type of account in more detail because many do not understand how they work and how you can benefit from them. These types of accounts are used for wealth building, retirement, and generational wealth because they work best over a long period of time.

But First, Some Financial Terms

Cash flow is a term that outlines how much cash is available to cover expenses. Every family needs cash to operate. In finance, cash flow refers to the amount of operating cash that "flows" through the family and affects the family's liquidity. You should review your cash flow monthly. Maintaining tight cash flow control is especially important if you live paycheck to paycheck.

Accounts payable represent your family's obligations to pay debts owed to lenders and creditors. Depending on the type of credit provided to your family, accounts payable can be short or long-term.

Accounts receivable is another term for money owed to your family by others for wages, interest, etc. Account receivables are never guaranteed and could disappear overnight.

Annual Percentage Rate (APR) represents the actual yearly cost of a loan, including all interest and fees. The total amount of interest to be paid is based on the original amount loaned and is represented in percentage form. When shopping for the right loan, you should know the APR for the loan in question. This figure can be beneficial when comparing one financial company with another since it represents the actual cost of borrowing. The interest rate and APR are two terms that are often used interchangeably, but they are not the same thing.

The interest rate is the cost of borrowing money, expressed as a percentage of the principal amount. The APR, on the other hand, is the total cost of borrowing money, including any fees or charges associated with the loan. The interest is the percentage of the principal amount you will pay each year. The APR, on the other hand, includes the interest rate and any other fees or charges associated with the loan, such as origination fees, closing costs, and mortgage insurance premiums. Sometimes, car dealerships will quote a low interest rate, but the APR is much higher because they bury their other costs in the loan so you do not notice it.

Compound interest calculations are complex and require software to figure it out. The actual calculation is $A = P(1 + r/n)^{nt}$. The variables are defined as follows:

- A is the total amount of money in the account after t years.
- P is the principal amount of money you initially deposited.
- r is the annual interest rate.
- n is the number of times the interest is compounded per year.
- t is the number of years the money is invested.

I will not expect you to follow all that. The critical thing to remember is that it works hard while you are sleeping. The key to compound interest is the annual interest rate (r), the number of times the interest is compounded per year (n), and the number of years the money is invested over time (t). So, let us look at an example calculated over 45 years.

You invest $200 every month at 9% for 43 years (age 22 to 68). After the first 10 years, not much appears to happen. Because you have the money coming out of your paycheck, you do not miss it or see it. After 25 years, you notice the number has jumped a lot. Then, after 45 years, you notice over $1,000,000 in your account. This all happens slowly over time based on exponential math. Remember we said that ROTH IRA accounts are already taxed, so that million dollars will never be taxed again during your retirement. Young adults should favor ROTH IRA accounts because they are portable as they jump from one job to another.

Don't Forget about Life Insurance

Some life insurance companies have exploited people for too long, offering products that have high commissions but do not pay out much upon death. I will not discuss companies or their products here but will cover why and when you should consider life insurance. Life insurance is important because it provides for lost income.

One of the primary reasons people get life insurance is to help ensure their loved ones will not face financial hardships if they pass away unexpectedly. Without your income, your family might be unable to afford your mortgage or cover tuition costs. Your life insurance death benefit can help pay for these because if you pass away with credit card debt or loans, the debt may not disappear. Someone will have to pay for it, depending on the state. In many cases, that could be your spouse and, if you are single, your parents.

Type of Investment Accounts

Stocks – When the price of a company's stock goes up, the value of the owner's investment in that company increases. The owner can choose to sell the stock for a profit or receive income via dividends. Buying individual stocks can yield huge gains but can also cause significant losses. Also, investing in individual stocks requires a lot of research and work. Most investors do not have that time, so they stick with stocks or mutual funds.

Bonds – These are considered safe and low-risk because the only chance of not getting your money back is if the issuer defaults. US saving bonds are backed by the US government, making them almost risk-free.

Mutual funds – This type of investment combines stocks and bonds. Mutual funds carry less risk because your money is diversified across many stocks and bonds, so they are probably the better option for the average investor who wants to realize gains without putting in much work.

Exchange-Traded Funds (ETFs) – These are similar to index funds in that they track a popular index and mirror its performance. Unlike index funds, though, ETFs are bought and sold on the stock market.

Certificates of Deposit (CDs) – CDs are an extremely low-risk investment, but with low risk comes low reward. Most banks offer CDs at a return of less than 2% per year, which is insufficient to keep up with inflation. People use these accounts when they fear losing money in the stock market. CDs are safe for a reason, but they do not build wealth.

401K – The significant benefit of this retirement option is that your employer may offer a "match," where they will put the same amount of money into your account that you put in up to a certain percentage. Because the investment is pre-taxed, you will get a reduced amount taken out of your check. Let's say your tax rate is 25%. Taking out $100 pre-taxed means roughly your check will go down by only $75. That, taken together with a company matching your first 6%, will get compounded over the years.

ROTH IRA —With both an IRA and a Roth IRA, you have more control over where you invest your money than a 401K. 401K accounts are controlled by the company you work for. With IRAs, you can invest the money in individual stocks, bonds, and mutual funds. The best news with Roth IRA accounts is that the retirement withdrawals are tax-free, forever. Knowing you don't have to pay taxes on this income will give you peace of mind and financial security.

Real Estate – You can make money by buying property at a below-market rate, selling it at a fair market price, or leasing the property to tenants. Some have made big money on "flipping" homes as a business model, where you buy, remodel, and rent or sell a home. Imagine buying four properties at $250,000 each with a 15-year mortgage, letting the renter pay off the mortgage, and then selling them for your early retirement. That is a cool $1,000,000 plus. Even better, imagine buying two properties every year for 10 years. That is an eye-popping $5,000,000, plus appreciation.

Key Takeaways

Charles A. Jaffe once said, "It's not your salary that makes you rich—it's your spending habits." In this chapter, we reviewed a lot about money, wealth, and credit. We focused a lot on investment accounts because that is where the secret to wealth building kicks in while you sleep. Of course, you could build wealth with real estate and start your own business, but those require you to work at them. Investing early in life is vital to using compound interest—if you have a career, max out your 401K or Roth IRA. Buying real estate is a safe strategy but is under pressure in 2024.

Change your relationship with money and keep some of what you make instead of spending it all each week. Everyone knows the quote, "It's not how much money you make but how much you keep." Make your money work hard for you, and do not continue to work hard for your money. Remember that bad credit means you pay more to borrow and may not get a job. Teach your kids how to manage money and invest, and if you are confused or need support, find a financial advisor to help you.

Your Next Steps

Learn more about compound interest, invest in your 401K at work, and use a ROTH IRA if you jump from job to job. You do not just want to invest; you want to maximize your contributions so your money can work magic.

In the next chapter, we will take on the controversial topic of breaking the cycle of poverty that affects millions of Americans.

Chapter 17 – Break the Cycle of Poverty

"Money is only a tool. It will take you wherever you wish, but it will not replace you as the driver."

Ayn Rand

In this chapter, we will explore if it is possible to break the cycle of poverty for some families. We know some families struggle and cannot consider investing in their future. Getting out of poverty is not an easy task or topic. However, some anecdotal things point us in the direction of hope. Rather than focusing on generational poverty, focus instead on finding $100 a month to invest to get a child out of poverty.

Question: Do you know people in poverty who have the latest iPhone?

Here are some anecdotal examples of spending that can be seen in distressed neighborhoods. The Classic Air Jordan sneaker runs about $2,000, while the Jordan Air 1 High runs $585. Nike Women's Air Zoom is $150. These are three common types of sneakers that many teenagers were wearing in 2021. One Grande cup of caffè latte coffee at Starbucks will run you $3.65 each—that is $113 per month and doesn't even count the blueberry muffin. Taking children to McDonalds these days is not cheap either.

Now, I am not here to judge; we know that many impoverished families do not buy these items. Unfortunately, many families do, and they do not realize how that monthly investment of $100 is achievable. In Chapter 15, we discussed the importance of making a monthly budget and tracking your monthly spending. Without a budget, families will not see where the money is going or realize how quickly $100 adds up to potential savings. For a young adult saving early, the magic number is $240 invested each month to hit $1,000,000 by the time you retire.

The Rich Uncle or Grandma Option

One of my favorite tactics for breaking the cycle of poverty is to ask wealthy family members to help get a child out of poverty. Every family has a rich uncle, aunt, or grandma. They are the ones who spoil your child and buy them expensive electronics, like video game systems. You should schedule a meeting with them and tell them what you are trying to do for the child's sake. Ask them to put half the money they spend on your child into the child's ROTH IRA account (a child must earn money, so we'll cover that later). Grandparents are another great source of help getting a child out of poverty. We are not talking about getting the parents out of poverty because it may be too late for them. We are focusing on the next generation.

The IRS rules allow children to start their own ROTH IRA as long as they have earned income. I have read over a dozen examples of rich social media coaches using their children and other family members to create earned income, so let's look at some examples. First, an aunt has an LLC company that does digital marketing for social media sites. She takes pictures of her kids or other family members on behalf of her LLC. She then writes a check for the services rendered, and the child receives earned income for the picture. She paid $600 for two photos to be used in her business. That is the $1,200 we needed from above.

Our second example comes from Grandma, who lives in the same neighborhood as her grandchildren. She has a dog and pays an 8-year-old

$10 to walk her dog in the mornings and again in the evenings. $20 per day for 30 days is $600 per month, and that is over $7,000 per year. If Grandma wanted to help a family escape poverty, this could be a targeted way to do it with earned income. Before you get concerned about tax forms, earned income below a certain amount does not require a tax return.

I will spend more time on how to make money in Chapter 18 because young people have more options to start a business today. Why? Older folks do not want to do anything themselves and have the money to pay someone else to do everything for them. I made good money as a kid pulling a lawnmower across town to cut grass or rake leaves. If you do not believe me, look out your window. How many people do you see cutting their grass in the summer or shoveling their snow in the winter?

Many Americans have gotten lazy and do not want to do anything. Some poor children have lazy neighbors within blocks of them who will pay them to do just about anything. We are not talking about child labor because babysitting, raking leaves, shoveling snow, walking dogs, and other minor tasks are supported by law.

Live within Your Means

The other approach is to look back at your budget and find the $100 per month, which is half our millionaire example earlier. $1,200 per year gets you a long way. If Grandma puts in $500 per year and the rich uncle puts in $500, then we are short $200. Consider Netflix, Amazon Prime, HBO, Starbucks, Olive Garden, upgraded iPhone, and Jordan sneakers, and you get the idea. Next time you drive through a poor neighborhood, look for Mercedes and BMWs.

Unfortunately, social media and hip TV shows have given a false impression that high fashion and beauty products are required to achieve respect and success. Most wealthy people do not waste money on expensive cars, fancy clothing, or grand vacations. Even hip-hop stars look a certain way on TV but live a modest lifestyle when the cameras are turned off. They learned the lesson that money makes more money only in equity form, and if money is in the expense form, you are making others rich. In Part 6 of this book, we will discuss examples of fake celebrity living.

So, ask yourself, do you need to get a new weave every month? Those fancy nails could last much more than a week. Guys will drop thousands of dollars on wheels for their cars or a banging stereo for great sound without considering the fact that others are getting rich from their money.

Now, let's be honest about something. Most people do not have the willpower to save 20 to 30% of their income for retirement. The critical point is that starting early in life only requires saving 5 to 10% of your income for a great retirement.

Key Takeaways

In this chapter, we touched on a sensitive topic. Getting children out of poverty is not easy, and I do not want to suggest that it is. I only provide alternatives in this book to help young people and their parents find other ways to be successful. We explored new strategies for bringing in rich family members to help and refocused on wasteful spending, and if any of these seems encouraging, then go for it.

Your Next Steps

Complete or review your budget for ways to find $100 per month to invest. Schedule a meeting with grandparents and explain how they can help get your child, their grandchild, out of poverty. Speak with someone who understands accounting and the income limits for earned income. Last, find a family member with a business and ask them to use your child in their marketing efforts. The reality is that wealthy families have been doing this forever.

In the next chapter, you will learn how to start your own business and consider how doing business in the 21st century has changed.

Chapter 18 – Start Your Own Business

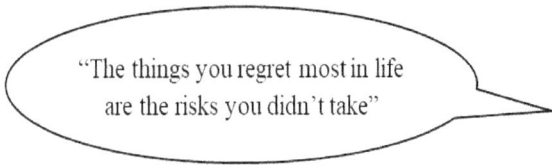

"The things you regret most in life
are the risks you didn't take"

Lewis
Carroll

In this chapter, we will explore why starting a business may be a good plan for young adults. Baby boomers, Gen X, and millennials believed that going to college, working for a great company, and retiring after 40 years was a successful plan. That model of work has been shattered and may not work in the 21st century, as we noted in Chapter 14. In past generations, if you wanted to start a business, you would work hard for a company while saving money and planning for your dream business. Most likely, that day never came because life got in the way. Relationships, children, buying a home, and getting promoted provide easy excuses for why the time was not right to launch your business.

In the 21st century, starting a business is easy. Technology, apps, and websites make it easy to plan, market, and sell your product or service. In most states, you can start a business for less than $300.

Question: Do you have a skill or talent that baby boomers will pay for?

Stepping out on Faith

In the old days, if you were strong enough to walk away from a steady paycheck and venture out, you needed to complete a few daunting processes. First, you needed a business plan outlining all aspects of your business idea and how you would run the company. It was so complicated that businesses charged lots of money to prepare your plan. You could use software to complete this plan when the technology cycle came along, but it still needed lots of information.

Second, you would need a financial plan outlining how you would finance the business in the short term as you waited for revenues to come in. This finance plan required you to present it to a bank loan officer, who would judge your idea and give you a yes or no. They had the power to kill your dream, and you had no option but to beg them for help.

Then came your marketing plan, where you documented your competition, your target market, how you would price your product or service, how you would advertise, and many other elements. You probably did not have the marketing skills, so you had no choice but to pay an expert to develop this plan for you.

So, What Changed?

Because the world's economic cycle has changed quickly over the past decade, you must consider how money is made in 2024 and beyond. Remember, Chapter 14 covered how people made money from the mid-1900s to 2023. They did it by using technology, information, and their brains to do what others did not want to do.

So, consider this point: Young people grew up with technology. They get, use, and share information on their phones, and they learn how to do things every day by watching YouTube, Tik Tok, and Instagram videos. Experts are sharing their knowledge using social media platforms so teenagers can learn from the best in the industry. We once called that being "an apprentice."

All of this has created a perfect storm for young people to start a business early in life and make money doing what others do not want to do. For example, many boomers and millennials want to start a podcast show to discuss topics of interest or to share their expertise. They love speaking into a camera but do not like to do the editing before uploading their show to YouTube or Spotify. Thousands of young people are making money today by doing the editing for a fee.

Everybody wins because the young person makes money working from home, and the older folks have extra money to pay for others to do the tasks they hate. This option is even more interesting because you can start a business for less than $300. The best part is you do not need a business or financial plan. You can even raise startup funds by doing a "GoFundMe" and raising $5,000 to launch your business.

Baby boomers must be pulling their hair out trying to understand how easy that is and how you can do business all by yourself. The marketing plan is still needed, but it is all digital. You can even pay someone a small fee to do the digital marketing for you by using a freelancer on Fiverr. You can do it yourself by using Canva to create all your digital marketing graphics and collaterals.

Social media is now the marketing medium of choice and only requires ad fees, which can be done for $10 per week. You can make your website without technical skills on Wix or GoDaddy and sell your product or service directly from your webpage. It does not get easier than that.

How to Start a Business

As mentioned earlier, starting a business in the 21st century is easier than ever. You can use large, specialized companies like Legal Zoom to handle all the work for you for a fee. That way, you do not have to worry about doing something wrong or making mistakes. If you are up to the challenge, completing the work yourself is not hard, so let us look at some requirements.

First, decide what **products or services** your business will offer. This decision may require you to collect and submit quarterly sales taxes to the state. If so, you will need a tax certificate from your state. Many young people are selling their knowledge as coaches or consultants, and you may need to consult with a CPA to determine tax requirements. We put products and services first because you must have a passion for your business.

Getting rich quick is usually not sustainable or enjoyable over the long term. If you are grinding and hustling all day, you won't have time to enjoy your hobbies or spend time with family and friends. You may be making lots of money but feel sad and lonely because making lots of money does not prevent depression. Therefore, you must be passionate about the product or service you offer in your business. It would help if you built your business around your life and passion—never build your life around a business.

Types of Business Structure

Next, decide on your **business structure**. A **sole proprietorship** is the simplest type of business. It is an unincorporated business owned and operated by one person who reports the business profits and losses on their personal tax return. However, you are personally liable for lawsuits and claims. A partnership is an unincorporated business owned and operated by two or more people who share the profits and losses according to a partnership agreement.

There are different types of partnerships, such as general partnerships, limited partnerships, and limited liability partnerships, which differ in the degree of liability protection and management authority for the partners.

A **limited liability company (LLC)** is a hybrid business structure created by the US Congress that combines the features of a corporation and a partnership. It is a separate legal entity owned by one or more members who have limited liability for the business debts and obligations. The members can choose how to manage the LLC and how to be taxed, either as a sole proprietorship, a partnership, or a corporation. Usually, members are protected against lawsuits. An LLC does not require a board of directors because the operating agreement serves that purpose.

An **S corporation** is taxed as a pass-through entity, meaning that the profits and losses are reported on the shareholders' personal tax returns, avoiding double taxation. An S corporation has one class of stock and no more than 100 shareholders, who have limited liability for the business debts and obligations. This type of business requires a board of directors.

A **C corporation** is the most common and complex type of corporation taxed as a separate legal entity. A C corporation can have unlimited shareholders, who have limited liability for the business debts and obligations. The profits of a C corporation are taxed twice, once at the corporate level and again when shareholders receive their dividends. A C corporation is the most complex and costly and requires a board of directors.

Because of their popularity and ease of management, we will focus on setting up an LLC business from here. Next, decide on your **business name**. You can research a business name on the secretary of state's website, and that step is critical because you want to ensure your business name is available. People should know what business you are in by your name.

Next, when selecting your business name, look for your business's website and social media handles. It is good practice to do these at the same time so you can reserve these names for your brand. Services like Wix allow anyone to create a website with little technical skills. You can watch YouTube videos on how to set up a Facebook or Instagram page.

Next, you will need a registered agent, a **business address**, a business phone number, and an email address. You must keep your business separate from your personal life, so get a virtual address online for less than $20 per month. You can get a business phone number for a small fee using an online phone service. Some people like to use Google Voice because it is a free phone service with a separate business number for calls and text messages. Most smartphones can have two phone numbers using an eSIM card. All major cellphone carriers offer these eSIM lines for around $10 per month.

Next, you must file your **articles of organization** with the state. Filing is done online and is simple. You can get a template for your LLC operating agreement online and then run it past a lawyer for the fine print.

Next, once the state has approved your articles of organization, you must apply for a business **Employer Identification Number** (EIN) from the IRS. Getting a free EIN takes about five minutes online and requires information from your articles of organization to complete this simple step. You will get your number immediately after submitting your application.

Next, apply for county, state, and local **business licenses**. Your secretary of state's website lists the requirements and where to get more information. Do not forget that tax collection is your responsibility if you sell taxable products. That means you will need a tax certificate from the state.

Next, you may need to give **public notice** in the local newspaper where your business address is listed so the community knows you are operating under that business name.

The last step would be to file your first **annual registration** with the state. You must do this yearly to confirm your business is still operating in the state. Congratulations, now your business is up and legal. If this seems like a lot of steps, use a company like Legal Zoom that will handle everything for a modest fee. Also, if you need hands-on support, my coaching business is here to help you start your business. We can do many of the above activities for you. We can also set up your credit card billing account and social media pages and create your website. Contact us at advisor@tips4living.org.

Operating Your Business

Now that your business is set up, a few things are left to complete. First, take your article of organization and your EIN and open a **business checking account**. You must keep your business money separate from your personal money. Do not forget to set up an **accounting system** to track all business income and expense line items.

Next, set up a **merchant account** to handle credit card processing. PayPal, Stripe, Clover, Square, and others are great options for billing your clients. Gone are the days when you had to pay thousands of dollars to handle credit card payments.

You will still need a **marketing plan,** but most small businesses use social media, email marketing, and their website for many marketing needs. There are freelancers who will create your business graphics for a small fee. Of course, you can do it yourself using a website like Canva.

In Figure 9 below, I list several ideas for marketing your new business. There are many other ideas to use, so ask ChatGPT to give you a complete guide to business marketing.

Figure 9

New Ways To Market Your Business

Get social media marketing training from YouTube

Set up free social media accounts

Pay a Fiveer freelancer to create a logo and brand kit

Pay a Fiveer freelancer to create a launch video for your business

Create a free 'lead magnet' to offer website visitors to get their email

Build a large email list to use with email marketing

Set up an expo table at a women's conference

Use a nonprofit or foundation to get a grant to pay for your marketing expenses

Let me end this business section with two examples of businesses teenagers can run to make money. First, Janet walks the family dog daily and loves pets. She notices a middle-class neighbor who seems unhappy walking her dog in the cold, so she gets permission from her mother to walk other dogs. Janet tells the neighbor that she could walk her dog in the morning for $10 and again in the evening for $10. The baby boomer neighbor is ecstatic to have someone she trusts to walk her dog and thinks 20 bucks is okay. Janet thinks to herself, *I can walk five dogs at a time*, so she approaches four other neighbors. Before long, she is walking six dogs. $20 x 7 days x 5 neighbors = $700 per week. That equates to $35,000 per year with two weeks of vacation with her family.

The second example is for teenagers who grew up with technology and love to edit videos for social media. John hears from his mother that a neighbor wants to start a podcast to share her experiences after 35 years as a music instructor at school. He has his mother ask around and find 14 other neighbors in his 500-home community who want to start a YouTube channel or a podcast but do not like the technical stuff. He offers to edit their recordings for $50 weekly and upload them to Spotify or YouTube. The women have done well with their retirement planning and are happy to do what they love without the "computer stuff" and agree to have John help them. $50 x 15 neighbors = $750 per week. That equates to $39,000 per year. John does not need to take two weeks off because he can do the work while on vacation with his family over breakfast. After all, it only takes him 30 minutes to do each edit, so he does them poolside.

Now, you may think those two examples sound too easy. But millions of people do not want to do things themselves, and they have disposable income to spend or are just lazy. Both the examples above should only require working part-time during the week, and they could double their income by getting more customers and spending their time pursuing their passions and hobbies. Assuming they have identified their five friends from Chapter 13 and have someone close to them, they will likely never be depressed.

The Concept of "Six Streams of Income"

The idea of having six income streams has caught on in the 21st century as a way of getting extra income and as a safety value for getting laid off. The essence of this book is to pursue a life of passion and purpose, and by now, you should be more comfortable filling in the blanks and determining how you will achieve that. Developing your skill set and preparing for the next economic cycle will ensure you stay calm and have a joyful life. However, if you believe in the idea of the "hustle society," read on because we will discuss how to achieve multiple income streams.

The concept of multiple income streams is a financial strategy that aims to diversify your means of income and reduce the risk of relying on a single paycheck. The idea is to generate income in different ways, such as work, business activity, investments, and royalties, so you can have more financial stability and independence. One common way to categorize the types of income streams is to put them into active and passive income buckets.

Active income refers to income that requires your direct involvement and hard work, such as working a job, running a business, or providing a service. Passive income refers to income that does not require your active involvement, such as earning interest, dividends, money from online courses, rental income, or royalties from your investments or writing a book.

You may have more than six income streams, while others may have less. The number of income streams is not as important as their quality and diversity. The goal is to create multiple streams of income that are consistent, scalable, and aligned with your financial goals and values.

Creating multiple streams of income can be challenging but also rewarding. It can help you achieve financial freedom, increase your net worth, and pursue various passions. However, this process requires careful planning and management. You need to consider your skills, interests, resources, risk tolerance, and the tax implications of each income stream.

You must also balance your time and effort between your income streams to avoid spreading yourself too thin. Remember, in Chapter 11, we discussed having balance in life and allocating time for family, friends, and hobbies so you can wake up smiling every day.

Example of Multiple Income Steams

Let us look at some 21st-century ways of having multiple income streams. Person A could work a full-time job, earn income from a published book on Amazon, do freelance writing, host a website offering online courses for $49 each, earn income from ads on a bi-monthly podcast show, charge others $97 to coach them on hosting a podcast, earn income from speaking engagements, and get income from affiliate marketing deals on their podcast and website. Person A would have eight streams of income. Interestingly, they could be making more in two of their passive income streams than they make in their full-time job at work. If they were to get laid off, they would simply keep it moving without getting stressed out about it.

Person B gave up working full-time for a company. They now own a lawncare business, own two rented real estate properties, provide handyman services, have a YouTube channel, and host a podcast and a blog where each gets ad revenues or affiliate marketing income. They have seven streams of income. Once the rental properties are paid off, that passive income could help them retire early and live without worrying about inflation or the economy.

You could say that both Person A and Person B are working too hard. I agree with you, but that is what the "hustle society" is all about. The key thing to remember is that they could reduce their income streams by half and still have financial security. Assuming that Person A and Person B invested in a 401K or ROTH IRA, they could easily be millionaires before age 50.

The two examples above are for illustration purposes only, but you can find many young folks on social media who are millionaires doing these types of things. If your goal is to make lots of money, you have all the advantages of technology, AI, information, and many wealthy baby boomers to drive your passions.

If your goal is to live your passion and use your talents fueled by your developed skills so that you are happy and joyful, then the earlier parts of this book showed you how to accomplish that. No stress or drama will exist for you because you want to impact the world and money is not your primary goal.

Key Takeaways

We started this part of the book by discussing changing your relationship with money. This included explaining how you could build a great credit score and budget to live within your means. Covering the fundamentals of money, we reviewed key financial terms and definitions. Additionally, we introduced the big wealth secret of compound interest and showed you how millionaires are made while working full-time. We explained the different types of investment accounts and the risks and rewards of each type, and we even touched on the controversial topic of breaking the cycle of poverty.

In this chapter, we end Part 4 by advancing an argument that young people starting a business early in life is a good thing. While parents and teenagers are questioning the value of a college degree, we showed you how to start a business without a college degree. The last part of this chapter ended by reviewing the concept of multiple income streams and how young people can do more than one thing in a week to make money.

In the end, you need to be clear about your future. Do you want to win the rat race and hustle all day, or do you want to pursue your passion and enjoy life while making a living?

Your Next Steps

You and your parents should schedule a meeting to discuss what was in Part 4. Because we are talking about money, you must discuss this with your parents and not just your friends. Many ideas and concepts may be controversial and require open discussion and input.

Do not forget to speak with your mentors about these concepts because they have experience in some areas. Schedule a meeting with your business and finance mentor because they are responsible for helping you with these matters. And remember, if you need hands-on help, I am an email away at advisor@tips4living.org.

Last, write down your conclusions and update your goals.

Part 5

Build, Live, and Share Your Legacy

PART 5 | Build, Live, and Share Your Legacy

"The purpose of life is to contribute in some way to making things better."
— Robert F. Kennedy

Kobe Bryant, the legendary NBA player, is a modern-day example of someone whose legacy continues to be shared after his passing. Beyond his remarkable basketball career, Kobe made an impact through storytelling, winning an Academy Award for his animated short film *Dear Basketball*. His Mamba Sports Academy and children's book series further showcase his commitment to inspiring others, particularly young people. Even though Kobe tragically passed away in 2020, his legacy endures through his contributions to sports and entertainment and his positive influence on aspiring athletes and creatives worldwide.

In the first four parts of this book, we covered recognizing your talents and passions, preparing for success by developing skills, living a purpose-driven life, and changing your relationship with money. In each chapter, we covered many things and discussed how to implement your decisions. Before this book comes to an end, we have to discuss how you want the end of your life to look. Let me remind you that "keeping the end in mind" is the best way of ensuring you reach your definition of success.

So, let's reflect on your legacy. You'll want to start this part of the book by answering a fundamental question: How do you want people to remember you when you are gone?

Most people will not reflect on this question until they are near the end of life or in the hospital receiving critical care. But if you can answer this question honestly early in life, you can live your legacy. How cool would it be for family and friends to know your legacy because they watched it year after year?

In Part 5, we will review what a legacy is and why you should care about yours. You will better understand how you will help others or solve a problem faced by others. Chapter 21 will give you specific ways to capture and share your legacy, and you will likely be surprised by many of our suggestions to capture and share your legacy because you probably never have heard many of these ideas. Our last chapter is packed with great ideas, just like the first chapter, because I promised you tips, ideas, and solutions that will change your life and give you the tools to coach others in a new way to succeed and be happy.

Use the Legacy Checklist in Figure 10 below and at the back of the book to capture items as you complete them.

Figure 10

Dare To Succeed Action Item Checklist

Action	Investment 1=zero 2=low 3=moderate	Status	Comments
Developing Your Legacy			
Self-Reflection and Identity			
Identify your values, principles and beliefs	1		use 'Skills to Passion Assessment Model'
Identify your natural talents given by God	2		use 'Skills to Passion Assessment Model'
Identify your passions	1		use 'Skills to Passion Assessment Model'
Identify the personality you want to have	1		
Develop a personal mission statement for your life's journey.	1		
Goal Setting			
Define personal and professional goals.	1		use goal tracking form
Break down goals into mini goals	1		use goal tracking form
Develop your milestones to check on progress	1		use goal tracking form
Personal Growth			
Identify skills development opportunities for your PDP.	2		use personal development plan form
Develop a schedule to meet with mentors	1		
Budget for continuous learning and skill development.	2		classes can be done online for free
Develop a routine for requesting personal feedback	1		
Cultivate a growth mindset.	1		
Relationship Building			
Foster positive and meaningful connections with family, friends, neighbors and mentors.	1		
Develop a schedule for contacting loved ones	1		
Learn negotiating skills	1		classes can be done online for free
Learn problem solving skills	1		classes can be done online for free
Health and Well-being			
Develop a physical fitness plan	3		gym membership, exercise equipment
Develop a mental health improvement plan	2		doctor visits, vacation plans, hobbies
Develop a plan for spiritual health improvement	1		Church, yoga, meditation
Develop methods for taking time outs or breaks from things	1		
Develop and maintain healthy eating habits.	2		vegetarian or vegan eating styles
Helping Others and Giving Back			
Volunteer at organizations that align with your values.	1		
Donate to charitable nonprofits.	3		
Write a book on an expertise you developed after 20 years	2		self-publishing is easier to get started
Start a blog or podcast to share your knowledge	2		
Mentor a teenager or young adult	1		

Chapter 19 – What's a Legacy?

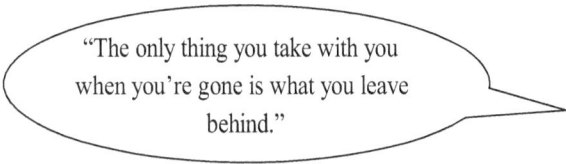

"The only thing you take with you when you're gone is what you leave behind." — John Allston

In this chapter, we explain what a legacy is and why defining yours early in life is crucial. Most people never think about a legacy until death is knocking on our door. Unfortunately, that is the wrong time to think about your life, what you did well, and who you spent time with. At the end of life, you do not have time to spend time with loved ones, serve others, start a business, be a better parent, improve your marriage, or implement any of your dreams.

Having a legacy is not about bragging about your accomplishments or how much money you have but about being thoughtful about the life you want to live. You cannot take your possessions with you, but you can take comfort in knowing that people remember you as one who impacted their lives. One of the best ways to make an impact is to set an example and be a role model of excellent behavior. Others are watching you, and some will do what you do and live how you live. You can impact others, even those you never meet.

Denzel Washington reminded us that we never see an armored car behind a hearse. You can't take money with you, but you can leave memories of your impact behind. The best thing you can do is help someone else. So, you have to decide if you want to make a positive or negative impact. Your impact is especially true with your children, who watch everything you do.

Question: How do you want people to remember you when you are gone?

What Is a Legacy?

A legacy refers to the lasting impact, influence, or contributions that you leave behind that shape the lives of others in a meaningful way. It includes the tangible and intangible things that endure beyond your lifetime, defining your impact on your family, friends, neighbors, and society as a whole.

Tangible aspects of your legacy may include physical creations such as books you have written, works of art, inventions, or a business you left for your children. These enduring items are concrete evidence of your accomplishments and contributions to your field of knowledge. For example, the scientific legacy of Albert Einstein, the theoretical physicist widely known as one of the greatest scientists of all time, helped future scientists create the technology we enjoy today.

Intangible aspects of your legacy are reflected in the values, principles, and ideologies you impart to family, friends, and others. This can include your influence on your community, the issues you fight to correct, or the positive changes you inspire in those around you. A caring person will influence others to be caring. Leaders and motivational speakers often leave a legacy of inspiration and empowerment that enables others to act and find their purpose.

Your achievements or public impact do not solely determine your legacy. Your legacy is defined by your character, ethics, and examples of doing good for the sake of good. You can leave a lasting legacy through mentorship, charity work, or acts of kindness by positively affecting the people and communities you touch.

In summary, your legacy is a multifaceted concept that represents the enduring impact of your life, encompassing both the tangible and intangible contributions that continue to resonate long after your death. Understanding, living, and sharing your legacy provides valuable insights into your life purpose and how you have influenced the world around you.

Why Have a Legacy?

Thinking about your legacy at a young age can offer several valuable benefits and help you shape a purpose-driven lifestyle. In Chapter 3, you thought about your passions and how you might find more joy and happiness doing what you love. Recognizing your passions not only gives you focus, but it also gives you motivation for taking action.

We mentioned that some college graduates find it challenging to find a job because the world changed during their four years of college. Defining your legacy can help you confirm your choices from Part 2 and Part 3 of this book, or it might cause you to update your plans altogether. Can you imagine how your goals might change after you define your legacy? You can change your goals as you live, but they cannot be adjusted after you are gone.

In the coming pages, we will review reasons why you might consider your legacy early in life so you can refine your purpose-driven lifestyle.

Clarifying Personal Values and Principles – Contemplating your legacy encourages deep thought and helps you define your principles and beliefs. By considering what impact you want to have on the world, you can align your actions and decisions with your core principles earlier in life.

Setting Long-Term Goals – Reflecting on your legacy can inspire you to set ambitious, long-term goals. Whether in college education, career, or personal development, having a sense of purpose and legacy-oriented goals can provide motivation and fulfillment. Setting these goals early in life will take the pressure off getting big things done. That way, defining your legacy early in life helps you avoid the midlife crisis faced by others who do not have a view of their legacy.

A midlife crisis is a period of emotional turmoil that typically occurs after 40 years old. During this phase, individuals experience a strong desire for change and begin questioning their accomplishments and life's meaning. People may question the value of their careers, hobbies, and relationships. These questions may be triggered by unresolved issues or coming to terms with their mortality. So, looking ahead and determining the kind of life you prefer may prevent these moments of crisis after you turn 40.

Building a Meaningful Life – Considering your legacy pushes you to think about how to lead a purposeful and meaningful life. A meaningful life may involve engaging in activities that satisfy you, contributing to the well-being of others, and leaving a positive imprint on the world. I believe that successful people must share their knowledge and experience with others, specifically guiding and developing younger generations rather than complaining about them.

W.E.B. Du Bois, the founder of the NAACP, wrote about the responsibility of the "Talented Tenth." He argued that providing higher education to a select group of people with intellectual and leadership abilities would empower them to uplift the people as a whole. He believed that by cultivating a group of well-educated and socially conscious people, they could serve as leaders and advocates for positive change within the broader African American community. Anyone who has gained knowledge and experience can help others succeed by applying this belief.

Creating Positive Habits and Behaviors – Awareness of your legacy can influence behavior and decision-making. Young adults who think about their impact on others and the world may be more inclined to develop positive habits, have better work ethics, cultivate empathy, and make choices that contribute positively to their communities. In the old days, young people would think about how their elders saw them and would work to improve their perceptions. Today, many people are debating whether teenagers and young adults are thinking ahead to their future and planning accordingly. This book provides a different approach to thinking about this question.

Fostering a Legacy of Relationships – Legacy is not just about your achievements but also about your impact on relationships and communities. As outlined in Chapter 13, you must be clear about your real friends and work hard to develop those lifelong relationships. Considering your legacy early on can encourage you to spend time and effort in building solid and meaningful connections with others.

Adapting to Changing Circumstances – Reflecting on your legacy allows you to adjust and evolve as the world changes. You can navigate life's challenges with resilience and purpose by staying true to your values, principles, and goals. This allows you to handle mental health challenges of hopelessness, anxiety, despair, and depression. Knowing your passions, gaining the skills to make money doing what you love, and knowing the legacy you want to leave behind are all guardrails against mental health issues.

Encouraging Personal Growth – Focusing on your legacy can drive continuous personal growth and self-improvement. You may be more inclined to seek learning opportunities, broaden your perspectives, and develop the skills necessary to make a lasting, positive impact if you live your legacy over a lifetime.

Key Takeaways

In summary, thinking about your legacy at a young age can serve as a guiding force by shaping values, principles, goals, and behaviors to contribute positively to your personal development and a purpose-driven lifestyle. It encourages you to lead a life of purpose fueled by passion that leaves a lasting, positive impact on the world.

Your Next Steps

Develop a personal mission statement that captures your values, principles, goals, and aspirations. This concise statement can serve as a guide, helping you stay focused on your legacy-building efforts. You can get examples of personal mission statements through a web search or ChatGPT. Your mentors, parents, and friends can help you with this task, but specifically your motivational and spiritual advisor from your success team should help you with your mission statement.

Think about living authentically true to your values and beliefs because authenticity resonates with others and contributes to a genuine and impactful legacy. Avoid compromising your principles for short-term gains. This exercise includes thinking about what personality you desire. A serious demeanor is good for some things, but others may consider you unapproachable. A fun-loving personality will get you a social life, but you may not seriously consider the life you want ten years from now. I am not favoring one versus the other, but I am bringing to your attention that being authentic, transparent, trustworthy, and honorable requires thought.

In the next chapter, we discuss how you can help others as part of your legacy.

Chapter 20 – Decide How You Will Help Others

"The best way to find yourself is to lose yourself in the service of others."

Mahatma Gandhi

In this chapter, we look at the power and responsibility of helping others as part of your legacy. Helping others has many benefits, but one of the greatest is the impact on our joy and happiness. Far too many people say they cannot figure out how to be happy due to all the issues of life and the drama of interacting with others. They do not realize that happiness comes from within, not from outside. Many life coaches help people understand they must work on being a better version of themselves before they can be a great person for someone else. Your heart confirms how you feel about yourself, but your soul confirms how you feel about others. Therefore, there is a secret to happiness that comes from helping others.

MacKenzie Scott, the ex-wife of Amazon's CEO Jeff Bezos, has a giving philosophy that reflects an impatience to distribute her wealth. She believes in empowering the good works of others rather than imposing her agenda on nonprofits, and she supports initiatives that address disparities and uplift marginalized communities. Her generosity is unprecedented: She has granted over $15 billion to nearly 2,000 organizations in just five years.

Question: How many examples can you think of where you helped others in the past three years?

How Can You Help Others?

Now that I have your attention, let's look at several ways you can help others and gain joy for your heart and soul. Think about how you may actively serve others and contribute to your community. Whether through volunteering at church, mentorship, or charity, giving back creates a positive social legacy and addresses the needs of those around you.

You should actively seek opportunities to uplift and inspire others. You may have the chance to become the matriarch or patriarch of your family, which helps others live by excellent standards. Although you are young, family members may come to you for advice. You may have avoided this role, but accept the challenge, step up, and serve.

A great way to help and inspire others is to share your knowledge and experiences. Passing on wisdom through formal teaching, informal mentorship, coaching, writing a book, or starting a podcast contributes to a lasting legacy. If you are beginning your adult life, consider what topics you may want to share ten years from now. You will be defining your passions, gaining skills, and picking a purpose in life, so consider that others are struggling to do the same and you could help them through it. And yes, teenagers have knowledge and skills and a story to tell and can help others find success.

Some of you may want to start a nonprofit. Starting this type of business is easy, cheap, and does not have to be complicated. You can have one output, such as teaching teenagers how to build a great credit score or maybe helping others eat healthier since you became a vegetarian in high school. Pick charity activities that align with your values. Supporting causes you believe in can create a positive impact that extends beyond your lifetime.

Others may want to support an organization like Big Brothers Big Sisters because you have the work skills to coach a young person. Stop procrastinating and step forward because someone needs you. You have more knowledge than they do, along with the skills and experience to help them find their way in life.

How Can Helping Others Help You?

Helping others can profoundly affect your overall well-being and contribute significantly to your joy and happiness. Here are several reasons why assisting others is important and how it can positively impact your sense of fulfillment.

Confirms Your Sense of Purpose – Helping others gives you a sense of purpose and meaning in life. Knowing that your actions make a positive difference in someone else's life can provide a deep and lasting sense of fulfillment. Since you have identified your purpose-driven lifestyle, you should pick areas that align with your purpose.

Increases Your Empathy and Compassion – Engaging in acts of kindness and support cultivates empathy and compassion. Understanding and sharing your experience can enhance your emotional intelligence and strengthen your connections with people. According to the Merriam-Webster dictionary, "passion" refers to a "strong feeling of enthusiasm or excitement for or about doing something." Compassion means "to suffer together." Researchers define it as the feeling that arises when you recognize another's suffering and feel motivated to relieve it. Compassion is what drives relationships after the initial passion has worn off, shifting the focus to the other person's happiness. It becomes about what they want instead of what you want.

Positive Impact on Your Mental Health – Acts of kindness and generosity release neurotransmitters like dopamine, endorphins, serotonin, and oxytocin, which contribute to feelings of happiness and reduce stress. These neurotransmitters relax you and release anxiety.

Builds Stronger Relationships – Helping others fosters stronger connections and relationships. Whether through supportive friendships, family bonds, or community involvement, a sense of shared purpose enhances the quality of your relationships. Nothing is better at building a bond with people than expressing your passions and future dreams of a purpose-driven lifestyle. You can imagine how these topics can break the ice when starting a conversation with a new friend, and many marriages result from having a shared sense of purpose and passion.

Enhanced Self-Esteem – Contributing to the well-being of others can boost your self-esteem. Recognizing your ability to impact someone else's life will reinforce a positive self-image and a sense of personal worth. Achieving success using skills is the best way to boost self-esteem.

Stress Reduction – Engaging in acts of kindness and generosity is associated with lower stress levels because the body releases endorphin hormones. The positive emotions generated by helping others can counteract the effects of stress and enable you to focus on your goals.

Increased Happiness – Studies have shown that people who regularly engage in acts of kindness report higher levels of happiness due to the release of hormones in the body. The positive emotions experienced during and after helping others contribute to a sense of well-being. According to research, some countries with low financial security report higher happiness. The reason may be grounded in helping each other as a community because although they do not have money for a material lifestyle, they focus on helping each other.

Longevity and Health Benefits – Research suggests a generous and helpful lifestyle may increase longevity, and additionally, positive emotions associated with helping others can have physical health benefits. Most doctors require you to state whether you have an emotional support network of family and friends when getting an annual exam. The belief is that interacting with others and doing meaningful work reduces sadness and depression. So, if you live alone, helping others as part of your purpose-driven lifestyle can help you stay busy and minimize loneliness.

Christian Living and Scripture – If you are religious, you know that helping others is part of your faith. Witnessing the positive impact of your actions on others reinforces the desire to continue engaging in supportive behaviors, leading to an ongoing cycle of joy and fulfillment.

Key Takeaways

In this chapter, we discussed the importance of helping others. These choices become inspirational when children, grandchildren, and others get to review what you did to help the world. We covered examples of how you can help others and how this support helps you in return.

There must be something to learn from underdeveloped countries that report higher happiness than countries with excess money and wealth. The old saying that money cannot buy you happiness must be true. If you believe money can bring more joy, reflect on Part 4, where we covered money and business in the 21st century. We showed you how to become a millionaire by the time you retire.

Your Next Steps

Decide how you will help others. You can start a blog, podcast, or nonprofit or write a book about how you solved a problem. People of all ages can volunteer at a local charity.

Reflecting on how to help others will help you in return. Write down your examples of helping others so you can share them with others to inspire them.

In the next chapter, we will discuss why capturing your legacy during your lifetime is essential so you can share the important things with family and friends after you are gone. We will give you examples of how to capture your legacy over decades, ready for sharing later.

Chapter 21 – Share Your Legacy

"The legacy of heroes is the memory of a great name and the inheritance of a great example."

Benjamin
Disraeli

In this chapter, we will discuss and show you how to document your major life milestones and memories so you can share them with loved ones later after you are gone. Many families face challenges representing a loved one's life at their funeral. Family and friends may opt to say something about the person and convey how they lived a life beyond themselves, while others may show a video or slideshow to highlight life's fun moments.

All of those are great choices. We will add a few to that list so you may capture a rich and detailed look at a person's journey. Documenting your legacy over the decades involves capturing a rich tapestry of milestones, memories, and special life events, and incorporating technology into this process can provide innovative and lasting ways to share these moments with future generations. Technology helps the family tell your story and confirm that you lived a purpose-driven life. Let's look at 13 ways to share your legacy.

I provide a long list of ideas because you may prefer some over others. You may prefer using technology to capture high-quality photos, videos, and audio, while others may prefer handwritten journeys, diaries, and letters. Most people would only use two to three of these, but you have the choice. It is best to look at options from digital and non-digital solutions that can cover several generations within your family because young family members may prefer hearing your story differently than older ones.

Question: How important is it for others to know your true life story?

Examples for Capturing Your Legacy

Create a farewell video that captures what you want to say to family and friends at your funeral. Some people may not be comfortable doing this video, while others may prefer a message coming from them directly. This video is not a place for judgment or criticism. It aims to speak about how you lived and tried to make a difference in the world.

Create a memory book that captures key moments of your life. Use one double-sided sheet for each memory. Put one large photo at the top and your words below describing why this is important to you. The back side of the sheet has 16 smaller pictures of that event or memory. Each sheet can capture vacations, marriage, birth of a child, college graduation, or any other event that made you happy or sad and you want to save it. Over three decades, you may have hundreds of these double-sided sheets—each one preserves your memory of that moment.

Instruct your executor to order a book of these memories from Shutterfly for each family member so they have a hard copy. The executor would send all the sheets to Shutterfly to create a book. Create a folder called "Lastname Memory Book" inside the "Lastname Legacy" folder so you can upload each sheet to this folder. See Figure 11 below for an example of a memory sheet that goes in the book.

Figure 11

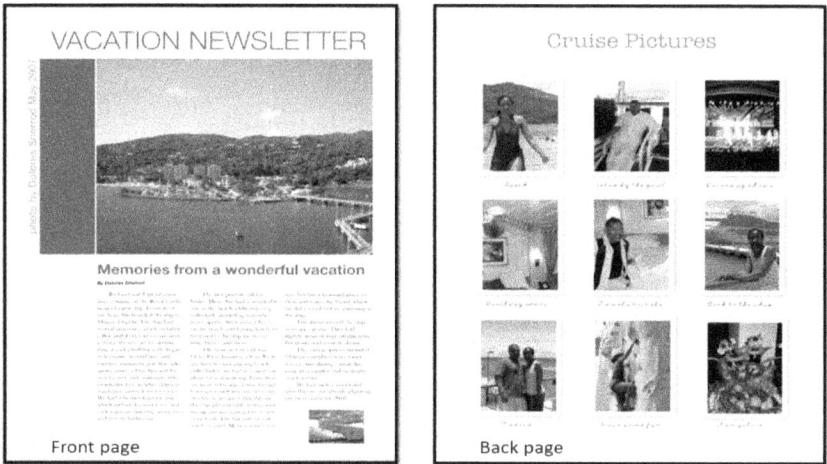

Instruct your executor to **create a 15-minute video of your life**. This video will feature you explaining things that are important to you, and it will include photos and video clips of key moments of your life. It will have your favorite song playing in the background and be fun and exciting to watch. Your executor may not have the time or skills to create this video, but do not worry. They can ask any 12-year-old family member to make it from the files provided in your "Lastname Legacy" Google Drive folder.

Record audio diaries to capture your voice, storytelling, and personal reflections so your loved ones can hear your emotions. Share anecdotes, memories, and insights in a format that preserves the emotional depth of your experiences. This option is suitable for older individuals who are uncomfortable in front of a video camera. You can use your smartphone to record the moments and upload them to your Google Drive folder called "Lastname Legacy." These audio files are short and recorded at the moment. Imagine the power of captioning your response to your daughter's first date or the birth of your grandchild.

I remember asking my mother what it was like for her growing up as a little girl in the old South, and she gave me what came to mind at the moment. But imagine if she had recorded some of those experiences when she was 17 or 25. Hearing the story in her voice during the year it happened would have been much better for me as her child who was over 50 years old at the time.

Over three decades, you could leave hundreds of these moments in your own voice. You could even record some of them for your friends so they know how you felt about them years earlier. Your executor will give them the password, so family and friends can listen to your audio diary.

Create a video podcast on YouTube to capture your voice, storytelling, and personal reflections. Because these are video files, they capture much more than audio-only files. Share anecdotes, memories, laughter, sadness, and insights in a format that preserves the emotional depth of your experiences. Podcast formats are also suitable for interviewing others on topics that are important to you. You can share your values, principles, beliefs, passions, and other topics in each episode, and capturing your views on marriage, parenting, work ethics, money, and other topics is a great way to leave guidance behind for younger family members. Name your video podcast "Lastname Legacy." You can host your podcast on Spotify and YouTube for free and make them private, requiring a password.

Write your autobiography. You obviously have many stories to tell, so why not share them in a book? This way, you can lay out details that family and friends may not know. It also allows you to clarify values, principles, beliefs, and suggestions for those who describe your life. For many, telling your story in a book gives you control over how your life story is told.

Create a website blog to capture your stories, explanations, and experiences. Blogs can contain words, photos, and videos. You can make the blog private as you collect a history of your life, and your executor can share the password with family and friends later. Many services offer a free website, so you will not spend money on these sites. Because they are free,

Sherrod – Dare to Succeed

they should be available long after you are gone without worrying about who is paying the monthly bill.

Use social media platforms to create time capsules. You can set up a private Facebook page to capture moments with videos, photos, and words. You can use features like Facebook Memories to revisit and share posts, photos, and status updates from specific dates in the past. After you are gone, your executor can change the private setting to public or invite family and friends to join the page.

Use digital scrapbooking tools to create visually appealing collages and albums that showcase major life events, celebrations, and milestones. Software like Canva can help design visually engaging digital scrapbooks. Canva is great because its AI can create slideshows from hundreds of photos, and this technology will save you lots of work when making the slideshow. You can then add short messages with each photo and save these scrapbooks to Google Drive for viewing.

Create a digital repository of photos, videos, and documents spanning your entire life. Use Google Drive to organize and catalog these visual memories, create a folder in Google Drive, and give viewing rights to anyone with the password. Add your password to the instructions for your executor who will handle your post-life matters. They will share the Google Drive link and password with family and friends.

Keep a digital journal to record daily thoughts, reflections, and significant events. This ongoing narrative can provide a detailed account of your experiences and the lessons learned throughout your life. A digital journal differs from a paper one because you can add photos and sound clips and make it accessible to anyone with your Google Drive viewing password. You can create a simple version of a digital journal by using Microsoft Word, Google Docs, or Apple Pages. Do not forget to save your documents as PDFs so others can view them from any device.

181

Document your family history using online genealogy platforms like Ancestry.com or MyHeritage. Include stories, photos, and documents about your ancestors to create a comprehensive family legacy. Download and save these files to your Google Drive folder.

Write letters to your family and friends expressing how you feel about them. You can express things you admire and respect about them and things that you learned from them. You can write about whatever you like because only the individual will see this letter. This practice is great because it is surprising how many friends are unsure of their true relationship with someone. They may have an idea, but a letter that clarifies their relationship would offer the friend joy and peace.

People need to hold onto memories of their friends, so a personalized letter could be a priceless gift. Upload the letters to a folder in your Google Drive and instruct your executor to share the letter with the individual only.

Key Takeaways

In this chapter, we discussed why it is important to share your legacy after you are gone. We provided 13 ideas for capturing and sharing your legacy in vivid detail, and this information will not surprise people who know you because they saw you live your legacy over the years. Do not let false information about you define how people remember you—you can control those perceptions by capturing the real you along your life journey.

All of these 13 ideas are free or low-cost. You can start today and document your life's journey using services like Canva, Google Drive, and YouTube. You can use your smartphone to receive audio and video on the go and edit these files using free apps on your smartphone. You can use free apps like Garage Band and Reaper.fm to edit audio and Microsoft Clipchamp and Apple iMovie to edit video.

Your Next Steps

Decide which of the 13 ideas you will implement. Do not forget to save your work to your Google Drive folder named for your legacy.

Chapter 22 – Lessons Learned

"By failing to prepare, you are preparing to fail." — Benjamin Franklin

As we wrap up our discussion about your legacy, let's reflect on how you lived your life and what lessons you may have learned. You may be asking, how can I do that since I have not lived my life yet? Don't worry because a scientific method might help. You probably have heard of the exercise where you look backward to recognize mistakes and successes from your experience. Looking back on life can generally be called "lessons learned."

In this chapter, you will reflect on life and ask yourself a simple question: What lessons have I learned over the past 40 years? One of the benefits of asking this question is that we can recall what went well and what went wrong as we made decisions and learned from experiences. This effect is called "hindsight is 20/20," meaning you can clearly see what went wrong after an event. This exercise allows you to make changes so you don't make the same mistake in the future.

You may have kept a journal of these events, which makes it easy to reflect on this question. But if you do not keep a journal, reflecting can help you remember key things you would do differently. You can do this exercise while you're young by thinking ahead. Ultimately, the best way to do this exercise is to ask yourself the thought-provoking question below.

Question: What would your "60-year-old self" tell your "30-year-old self" in hindsight?

20 Examples of What You Might Tell Your Younger Self

Invest in your health because your body is more fragile than you think, and you are not indestructible. Take care of your body by exercising regularly, eating a healthy diet, meditating to reduce stress, and getting enough sleep. I highly recommend Dr. Michael Greger's nonprofit, NutritionFacts.org, as a source of excellent health information. He offers free videos on hundreds of topics, each with health improvement ideas.

Save and invest early because the future will come sooner than you think. Being homeless when you are 65 years old is no joke, so do not take it for granted. Start saving for retirement just after high school or sooner and invest in a ROTH IRA. We covered the advantages of this type of investment in Chapter 16 and pointed out that it produces tax-free income. Your best money secret as a young person is "compound interest," and I covered examples of how your money can work hard for you in Chapter 16 using compound interest.

Build meaningful relationships because no one wants to be alone in retirement. In Chapter 13, we discussed the importance of cultivating strong connections with family and friends, and these relationships will be a source of support and joy throughout your life. According to doctors, this can also help you live longer—for example, some studies have shown that marriage adds 10 years to your life.

Don't sweat the small stuff because it is not that important at the end of the day. Life is full of ups and downs, so accept that you can't control several things, events, or people, and do not let minor setbacks and inconveniences ruin your peace of mind. Worrying about things you cannot control only adds stress, which is unhealthy. I live by the saying, "No one will die today due to my bad decision." That is true for about 80% of the population; however, with some jobs, you should worry about your decisions. For example, police, firefighters, doctors, nurses, and EMTs are jobs where a wrong decision could cost someone their life.

If you are not one of those professionals, others will forget your decisions shortly after you worry about the mistake. I highly recommend the short book *Who Moved My Cheese?* to understand this concept fully.

Take calculated risks because that is when the magic happens, and do not be afraid to step out of your comfort zone. Whether it is starting your own business or introducing yourself to a potential spouse, do not be scared because nothing good will happen if you take no action or try too hard to avoid a mistake. Some of the best opportunities come from taking calculated risks. We covered in Chapter 9 that great success can only come after failure and learning how to succeed.

Learn to say no because you only have 24 hours each day, and you must balance life's requirements. Prioritize your time and energy, and do not forget to prioritize your joy and mental health. It is okay to say no to things that do not align with your values or goals. It may be hard to accept that some friends may ask a lot of you but will not be there when you need them. We covered this in Chapter 13 and pointed out in Chapter 11 how to develop a lifestyle model based on a good balance.

Travel the world and explore your country. Visiting the world and experiencing different cultures allows you to grow because it will broaden your perspective and create lasting memories. You will not only have fun but may find your purpose in life. We discussed finding a purpose-driven life in Part 3 of this book.

Embrace failure as a way of learning how to succeed. Failure is a part of life, and great discoveries come from these moments of letdown. One of the lessons learned above is the importance of taking risks and embracing failures. You may do everything right but still fail because the universe is complicated, and it may not be your fault.

Live below your means because "keeping up with the Joneses" will make you poor. Avoid unnecessary debt, and do not spend money you do not have. Remember that using credit cards too freely is the best way to be financially insecure. Financial freedom brings peace of mind and hope for the future, and this freedom also helps you sleep better at night.

Focus on experiences and doing good for the sake of good, not owning more stuff. Material possessions come and go, but the experiences you accumulate, the close friends you nourish, and the good you do for others will stay with you forever. This also means putting the phone away and enjoying the moment—you could share a concert moment or a great vacation picture with others but may miss it for yourself.

I would be remiss if I left out your children's experiences. Working hard may be necessary, but do not forget that your children need you also. Be there to experience their moments of joy—they may not always remember when you were there, but they will remember when you were not. Ultimately, you only get one chance to live a moment in time, so do not take any day for granted.

Take care of your mental health, and do not assume that everything will be all right. It will be all right when you take steps to ensure it will be good. As important as your physical health, as covered earlier, you must be deliberate about your mental health. Despair, anxiety, hopelessness, and depression will only be under control if we take action, so do not hesitate to seek help if you are struggling emotionally.

Keep learning forever because the world is continuously changing. Stay curious and never stop learning because technology, cultural norms, financial stability, and our climate is changing every day. We covered the importance of continuous learning in detail in Chapter 14. If you do not change, you will be left behind.

Share love as a way of life. Do not get caught up in the past or future, but cherish the present moment and the people around you. Do not lose the ones you love because you took them for granted and did not tell them how much you love them. Far too many marriages fail simply because love got lost along the way.

Forgive and let go because holding grudges is unhealthy and does not solve anything. Holding onto grudges only weighs you down and causes distractions. Forgive, let go, and move forward. When you reflect on your legacy, you will regret not forgiving key people, including your enemies.

Celebrate your achievements because meeting a goal is a big deal. Take time to acknowledge and celebrate your accomplishments, no matter how small. Recognizing your hard work is essential, as it boosts your mental health, and do not forget to share the celebration with family and friends.

Make a difference in the world because it is not just about you. Time is a precious resource, so be mindful of how you spend it and prioritize activities that align with your goals and values. God gave you gifts and talents that others do not have. Share your experiences, skills, and knowledge with others as called for by W.E.B. Du Bois. We covered the importance of helping others in Chapter 20—some people find that helping others brings them the greatest joy and adds to their happiness.

Do not compare yourself to or compete with others. Everyone's journey is unique, so focus on your own path and celebrate the successes of others without feeling inadequate or jealous. What you do best, others do not, and vice versa—you can learn from each other if you respect and appreciate what they have to offer you in return for what you can offer them.

Effective bullying occurs when someone causes you to compare your looks, weight, skin tone, hair, clothing, or speech with someone else. Accept you as created by God, and stop comparing.

You cannot model your life after a celebrity and music icon. Most celebrities do not live the way you see them on TV, and we will cover this in Part 6 of this book. Comparing yourself to a celebrity is the best way to destroy your self-esteem, and it is also a quick road to financial insecurity, as the lifestyle requires lots of money.

Stay true to your values. Define your core values and live by them. Values will guide your decisions and bring authenticity to your life, and making choices based on principles will add meaning to your day. You may not know it, but others are changing for the better because they see you live by great values. So, set the example and do not let changing political or cultural extremes change how you live your life.

Live based on your passions. Everyone will tell you how to live and push you to make as much money as possible, but you know that money does not buy happiness. The greatest defense against bad mental health is to live a life based on what you love and enjoy doing. We spent lots of time on this topic in Part 1 of this book because I believe it is the missing secret to better joy in life.

Listen to your parents and loved ones because they want the best for you. Learning from mistakes takes time, money, and disappointment, but there is a shortcut to learning from mistakes, which is learning from others. You may think your parents do not understand or have not done much in life, but I assure you, they have "been there and done that." There are no new failures in life because someone has "been there and done that."

It is okay to question what they say, but you must listen before you can hear it. Sometimes, we must trust that they have skills and experience we may not know about.

Remember, life is a journey, and each day is an opportunity for growth and learning. Enjoy the ride!

Key Takeaways

In this chapter, we looked backward at lessons learned in life. By doing this exercise when you are young, you can change how you live in the future. There is no reason you cannot learn from the lessons of others to not make the same mistakes. If you do this exercise well and adjust some of what you wrote down in prior chapters, you may succeed sooner.

Your Next Steps

Consider all these examples above and decide if you need to change your prior decisions, goals, and plans.

Ask your parents, grandparents, aunts, and uncles to do this exercise so they can share their recommendations with you. Make changes as necessary.

Part 6

Don't Believe Everything You See on TV

PART 6 | Don't Believe Everything You See on TV

"Behind every red -carpet smile is a person with struggles you can't see" — Taylor Swift

In this chapter, we look at the stark contrast between the glamorous portrayal of celebrity life on TV and social media and the reality of life for young adults. The media, often portraying celebrities as an example of success and happiness, can inadvertently set unrealistic living standards for teenagers. Because of this, you must know the difference between fiction and reality and understand that celebrities' on-screen roles are created for entertainment—those TV roles are not a blueprint for living a successful life. Look beyond the illusion of celebrity lifestyles seen on screens when navigating the challenges of your own life.

What Is Wrong with Living Like a Celebrity?

Celebrities present a picture of fun-filled and happy lives through carefully created images and scripted roles. However, celebrities deal with their own challenges, insecurities, and problems behind the scenes. Realizing that nobody's life is without difficulties helps you embrace your own personality and unique journey.

TV and social media often portray celebrities living wealthy lifestyles, leading teenagers to believe that material wealth equates to happiness. Most celebrities do not live the life they portray on TV, and most of them also do not waste money on expensive material items as shown on TV. We will deal with these differences in the upcoming chapters.

Be aware that pursuing a lifestyle of fast-paced living, wearing designer clothes, driving expensive cars, and nightly partying will have a negative impact on your mental health. The constant comparison to idealized celebrity lives can adversely affect your self-esteem.

TV often depicts celebrity friendships as glamorous and drama-free, fostering the misconception that popularity and social status equate to genuine connections. But nothing could be farther from the truth—many celebrities, like Britney Spears, have written about fake friends and those who show up only to feed off their money. Instead, value authentic relationships and prioritize real connections over the pursuit of popularity.

The last point I will make is that celebrities employ teams of professionals to manage their public image. What you see on TV is a curated story, carefully constructed to appeal to audiences and make money, so you should develop a healthy skepticism and use critical thinking when consuming media. The stories and lifestyles are fake.

Ultimately, this part of the book serves as a guide for you to cultivate a realistic perspective on life, appreciating that happiness comes from embracing your authentic self and unique journey rather than emulating a fictionalized and unattainable celebrity lifestyle.

You should not model your lifestyle based on how celebrities live on TV and social media. In Part 6, we will cover the following topics:

- ✓ Celebrities don't live like the roles they play on TV
- ✓ Most wealthy people do not waste money living lavishly
- ✓ Expensive cars and clothes can put you at risk

Chapter 23 – Celebrities and Fake Living

"I've learned that success is not measured by the fame I've gained but by the authenticity I've retained."

Emma Watson

In this chapter, we point out how celebrities do not live the life they portray on TV because it is fake and created to entertain and make money. Unfortunately, many young people today believe in the big lie that success is hustling to make lots of money, wearing fancy clothes, driving exotic cars, traveling in private planes, and partying like a rock star.

They do not realize that most celebrities do not live that way in real life. When the paparazzi take an unplanned photo of them, you can see them wearing jeans and T-shirts, eating ice cream or pizza, and sunbathing at the beach. In other words, the celebrity is trying to live like you, an ordinary person, and get some joy out of the day. Meanwhile, you are busy trying to live the big lie of what you see on TV. In the process, you are going broke, losing real friends, losing your girlfriend or boyfriend, and getting depressed and emotionally unstable.

If you rent an apartment, why are you driving a BMW? You could be saving that $1,000 per month to buy a house.

Question: How many celebrities do you think are truly happy?

Stories of Celebrities Who Live Differently than They Appear on TV

Example 1

Beneath the Spotlight: The Hidden Realities of a Celebrity Star

Robin Williams, the brilliant comic mind with a soulful spirit, grappled with a lifelong battle against addiction and depression. Despite keeping millions of people laughing, his personal struggles were deep and often hidden from the spotlight.

In the late '70s and '80s, during the heyday of *Mork and Mindy*, Robin was known as a good-natured, gifted star. However, behind the scenes, he faced demons. He once confessed, "Do I perform sometimes in a manic style? Yes. Am I manic all the time? No. Do I get sad? Oh yeah." His struggles began soon after his rise to fame, fueled by the myth of living fast and dying young. Yet, he emerged on the other side, even as he continued to battle deep bouts of sadness. Behind the laughter, he carried the weight of depression, a silent companion that ultimately led to his tragic death.

Let's stay focused as we explore why teenagers should not idolize and emulate celebrities. Robin's journey reminds us that the truth of our view is often more complex than the polished story on screens.

Example 2

Unveiling the Princess: The Real Story of Britney Spears

Britney Spears reigned as the undisputed Princess of Pop in the fast-paced music world. Britney was the epitome of a global success story, from her breakout hit song "Baby One More Time" to her electrifying performances that captivated millions. However, behind the glitz and glamour of her public persona was a story of pain that few truly knew.

Her rise to fame was meteoric, catapulting her into the spotlight at a young age, and the world saw her as the quintessential pop sensation. Still, the reality was a journey filled with the challenges of navigating life as a young adult under the scrutinizing gaze of the media. As her career soared, so did the pressure of expectations, and fame took a toll on her personal life. The public witnessed a highly publicized relationship that went south for all the world to see.

Amidst the whirlwind of fame, Britney faced personal struggles that extended far beyond her catchy tunes and choreographed dance routines. She had a conservatorship imposed on her, understandingly for her well-being, that became a symbol of the limitations of living a wild lifestyle. It was not just a legal arrangement but a sharp reminder that the person behind the fame was fighting battles unseen by the adoring fans.

Her fight for autonomy shed light on the destructive elements of the entertainment world, where the pressures of being a celebrity can overshadow the very essence of humanity. She could see no joy, no happiness, and no future.

As the world chanted her name in sold-out arenas, her personal battles unfolded behind closed doors. Her story serves as a reminder that even the most celebrated stars are, at their core, vulnerable and deserving of joy and happiness, which often do not come from fame and wealth.

Thoughts from Celebrities to Consider

Behind the radiant smiles and dazzling performances, even the most celebrated stars grapple with the echoes of their own vulnerabilities.

Ethan Sterling reminds us, "The characters on screen are but fleeting shadows, and the real drama unfolds in the unscripted moments of everyday life."

David Bowie views fame this way. "I think fame itself is not a rewarding thing. The most you can say is that it gets you a seat in restaurants."

In the curated world of social media, Kylie Jenner reminds us that "what we see is a meticulously constructed narrative, a snapshot of a life carefully framed and filtered."

A lesson from the life of Emma Watson: "The applause may fade, but the impact one leaves through genuine authenticity and purposeful actions are timeless."

As Jennifer Lawrence once remarked, "The red carpet may be glamorous, but the real strength is the vulnerability to let your true self shine to others."

Key Takeaways

The Robin Williams and Brittany Spears examples serve as thoughtful reminders that the glittering celebrity lives seen on TV are often a mirage, concealing the difficulties and vulnerabilities that exist in every individual's life struggles.

As we wrap up this chapter, you should understand why you should not blindly emulate the fictional lives of celebrities. Instead, seek inspiration from the authenticity of your own experiences and aspirations, fueled by your unique passions, talents, and skills. Celebrity life is mainly fake, so you will never achieve happiness trying to live the life you see on TV.

Your Next Steps

Use the chapters of this book to develop your lifestyle based on your talents, passions, and skills. Be unique and enjoy each moment of life as a unique path just for you.

Evaluate your lifestyle to see if you are patterning your behavior based on the examples you see on social media or TV. Then, decide if you must change your choices, behavior, and lifestyle.

Chapter 24 – Wealthy People Don't Waste Money

"The truth is, no one has a perfect life, even if it looks like they do. You can't compare your life to someone else's highlight reel."

Bill
Gates

In the last chapter, we laid out the reality that celebrity life is fake and gave examples to illustrate the point. In this chapter, we look at the myths associated with wealth and spending. Far too many people live a life to please others and spend money to show what they have instead of who they are.

Some young adults think wearing the latest threads makes them desirable. Also, past generations thought driving the latest expensive car brands made them desirable. The reality is that no generation will be desired by the stuff they own, at least by honorable individuals. You should make enough money to buy what you need, not everything you want because your mental health is more important than buying everything you desire.

Respect and credibility come from your character, how you treat people, and the principles you live by, not from expensive cars, clothes, jewelry, and hefty bank accounts. The question below should make you think about how you live instead of how much money you have.

Question: Who would get more real friends, Tony Stark (Iron Man) or Tyler Perry (the movie producer)? Keep in mind that both are billionaires.

Examples of Wealthy People Who Do Not Waste Money

Warren Buffett

Despite being one of the wealthiest individuals in the world, Warren Buffett is known for his frugal lifestyle. He famously lives in the same modest house he bought in 1958, avoids extravagant purchases, and prefers simple pleasures like a McDonald's breakfast. His down-to-earth approach to wealth has become a hallmark of his philosophy.

Known for his long-term approach to investing, Warren believes in the power of compounding interest over time. An avid reader, he believes in the importance of continuous learning and allocates a significant amount of time to reading and acquiring knowledge, emphasizing that the more you learn, the more you earn. He places a high value on integrity and reputation.

Warren famously said, "It takes 20 years to build a reputation and five minutes to ruin it." This quote reflects the importance of honesty and integrity in all business dealings. In addition, he is generally cautious about using debt and encourages financial discipline. His philosophy is reflected in the advice that "The most important thing to do if you find yourself in a hole is to stop digging." Warren Buffett could buy anything in the world, but he does not.

Here are 12 things billionaire Warren Buffett says non-wealthy people waste money on (Fisher 2024).

1. **Neglecting Personal Development**: According to Buffett, the best investment one can make is in oneself. Enhancing skills and education can boost earning potential significantly. Knowledge and skills are assets that no one can take away.

2. **Relying on Credit Cards**: Credit cards can be convenient, but high interest rates can quickly overshadow any benefits if you don't pay the total balance monthly.

3. **Frequenting Bars and Cubs**: Spending on social activities like drinking at bars can add up. Opting for more affordable social gatherings, like home get-togethers, can help save significantly.

4. **Chasing the Latest Technology**: New gadgets may be tempting, but last year's model often serves just as well.

5. **Overspending on Clothes**: Choosing classic, durable clothes over flashy, expensive brands can result in significant savings.

6. **Buying New Cars**: Cars are notorious for their rapid depreciation. Buy pre-owned cars and hold onto them for as long as they're reliable instead of falling for the allure of the new models.

7. **Unused Gym Memberships**: You should be active, but be cautious against unused gym memberships. Free or low-cost fitness routines can be just as effective if regularly practiced.

8. **Multiple Screaming Subscriptions**: Subscription services can become a financial drain. A family only needs a couple of options.

9. **Over-Reliance on Skincare Products**: Finding a simple and effective skincare routine can save money and your skin.

10. **Regular Nights Out**: While socializing is essential, frequent nights out can be a significant expense. Opting for budget-friendly alternatives like home-cooked meals and movie nights can cut costs considerably.

11. **Gambling**: While gambling might seem like a shortcut to wealth, you must understand the odds. Instead, make financial decisions that favor long-term wealth accumulation, not momentary thrills.

12. **Smoking**: Beyond its health implications, smoking is a costly habit. Quitting can significantly boost your budget.

Mark Zuckerberg

Mark Zuckerberg, the co-founder and CEO of Facebook, is recognized for his relatively modest lifestyle. Despite his immense wealth, he famously drives an affordable car, lives in a comparatively modest home, and focuses on philanthropy through the Chan Zuckerberg Initiative. You will not find him partying the night away and dropping money on the latest fads.

He believed in the idea of "Move Fast and Break Things." This mantra was a guiding principle in Facebook's early days, emphasizing the importance of rapid innovation and a willingness to take risks.

The idea was to prioritize progress over perfection, acknowledging that mistakes and failures are inherent in the process of innovation. Mark believes that focusing clearly on your mission helps guide decision-making and maintain your long-term vision.

Ingvar Kamprad

Ingvar Kamprad, the founder of IKEA, was known for his thrifty lifestyle. Despite being one of the wealthiest people in the world, Kamprad drove a Volvo, flew economy class, and stayed in budget hotels. His commitment to a modest lifestyle mirrored the values he instilled in his business, which was to not waste money. He valued the lessons from failure and saw them as opportunities for improvement and growth.

Tyler Perry

Tyler Perry, the highly successful filmmaker, playwright, and actor, is known for his climb to billionaire status and a notably modest lifestyle. He doesn't indulge in lavish spending on personal luxuries, often dresses casually, and has been spotted driving inexpensive vehicles. His down-to-earth approach to personal lifestyle choices reflects his commitment to living modestly. Despite his fame and wealth, he maintains a hands-on work ethic. This commitment to actively engaging in his work aligns with his modest, disciplined approach to success.

While he has achieved significant financial success, he is also known for his charity work and giving back to the community. Tyler Perry's lifestyle and financial decisions reflect a commitment to humility, practicality, and community. His success has not led to extravagant living but rather to a deliberate and mindful approach to wealth management. One thing he did do, which many people agree with, was buying real estate. If you need to sink money into something, buy a great house.

Steve Jobs

Steve Jobs, the late co-founder of Apple and the iPhone, was known for his minimalist lifestyle. Jobs wore his signature black turtleneck and jeans and lived in a relatively modest historic mansion in Palo Alto, California. Despite his success with Apple, he focused more on the impact of his work than on amassing extravagant personal wealth. He once stated, "Innovation distinguishes between a leader and a follower," emphasizing the importance of pushing boundaries to create transformative products. Steve faced numerous setbacks in his career, including being ousted from Apple in the 1980s. However, his resilience and determination were evident as he returned to lead the company to unprecedented success.

His philosophy included the idea that setbacks were integral to any entrepreneurial journey. He had a profound focus on leaving a lasting legacy, and he aimed to create products that would significantly impact people's lives and change how they interacted with technology. This legacy-focused philosophy is evident in Apple's continued influence on the tech industry.

Examples of Wealthy People Who Wasted Money and Went Broke

MC Hammer

The famous rapper and entertainer MC Hammer experienced significant financial challenges in the 1990s due to extravagant spending. His massive success with hits like "U Can't Touch This" and "2 Legit 2 Quit" led to a lavish lifestyle, including a large entourage, luxurious homes, and a private jet. However, his spending habits outpaced his income, and he filed for bankruptcy in 1996. If you read his story, you know many people called themselves his friend—they went to parties with him and declared themselves loyal until he was broke. Then, the fake friends all disappeared.

Mike Tyson

The former heavyweight boxing champion, Mike Tyson, faced financial ruin despite earning hundreds of millions of dollars during his career. Mike's financial troubles were attributed to lavish spending on mansions, cars, extravagant gifts, and a series of legal problems and divorces. In 2003, he filed for bankruptcy, and at one point, he owed tens of millions of dollars to creditors. He has since worked on rebuilding his financial life through various endeavors, including acting and public appearances. He often speaks about the mistakes he made with money. I can only imagine that he would do things differently in hindsight.

Lindsay Lohan

Lindsay Lohan, a once-prominent actress, faced financial difficulties due to a combination of legal troubles, substance abuse issues, and a reportedly extravagant lifestyle. The star of films like *Mean Girls* and *Freaky Friday* experienced financial strain as her career took a downturn. Legal fees, rehab stints, and personal expenses contributed to her financial challenges. While Lindsay's financial struggles may not be as high-profile as some other celebrities, they reflect the impact of a lavish lifestyle coupled with personal and legal issues on one's financial stability and mental health.

Nicolas Cage

Nicolas Cage, the Academy Award-winning actor, faced significant financial troubles in the mid-2000s, leading to a series of high-profile financial setbacks. Cage, known for his roles in films like *Leaving Las Vegas* and the *National Treasure* series, reportedly accumulated an extensive real estate portfolio, including castles, mansions, and unique properties. His lavish spending habits and a series of legal issues and tax problems led to financial difficulties. He faced foreclosure on several properties and owed substantial unpaid taxes.

In an effort to address his financial woes, he sold numerous assets, including rare comic books and his dinosaur skull. Despite these setbacks, he has continued his acting career and improved his financial situation. Cage's story serves as a cautionary tale about the importance of financial management, even for high-earning professionals.

Key Takeaways

In this chapter, we discussed the importance of making enough money to buy what you need, not everything you desire. We showed five examples of wealthy people who do not waste money on the latest luxuries of the world. Instead, they focus on generational wealth and not on living big today.

We could have given you 20 examples of wealthy people who spend big and live large. However, some people that come to mind are now broke and struggling to make ends meet. One of our examples was Mike Tyson, a hard-working man who made millions of dollars only to spend too much and lose it all. His so-called friends were nowhere to be found at his lowest point in life. Mike showed us that it is not how many times you get knocked down but how many times you get up and try again.

If you are lucky enough to make a lot of money, focus on keeping much of it. A common quote suggests, "It's not how much you make, it's how much you keep." Frequently, people with less try to live wealthy, while people with wealth try to live with less.

So, next time you buy Jordan sneakers for $2,000, the latest Mercedes for $100,000, or fly first class, ask yourself if you are making others wealthy instead of building generational wealth for your family.

Consider this: Many people who inherited their wealth live a lavish lifestyle because they didn't earn the money and can't appreciate the hard work involved in getting it. Most people who grew up poor or middle class and then became wealthy do not spend lots of money on material things because they worked too hard for that money and appreciate what it took to get it. They have no intent of losing their money through luxurious spending and making other people rich.

Your Next Steps

Reflect back on Part 4, Changing Your Relationship with Money, and develop a philosophy where you can build wealth instead of living wealthy. For the best result, discuss this with your parents, friends, and mentors for input.

Chapter 25 – Luxury Cars and Items Are Risky

"In the age of social media, everyone is a brand. But remember, authenticity is your greatest asset."

Oprah
Winfrey

In this chapter, we will discuss a topic we see in the news every day involving robberies targeting people flashing expensive items. In your quest to be like Cardi B or Jay-Z, you are putting your life at risk because criminals are watching. There are too many stories on TV where a teenager was robbed or shot when crooks stole their Jordan sneakers. Walking the streets while speaking on the latest iPhone, wearing expensive jewelry, or even wearing that designer handbag will make you a target.

Unfortunately, crooks don't just steal your expensive items—they sometimes use handguns to kill in the process. And unlike Cardi B, you do not have a security detail to protect you from harm. Therefore, think twice before flashing expensive items.

Question: How many news stories have you heard where luxury cars were taken at gunpoint?

Instagram is a one-stop shop for thieves who can easily browse content from influencers around the globe and choose their next targets. With wealthy celebrities' IG feeds dotted with pictures of luxury cars, expensive handbags, and multiple homes, they act as expensive inventory for those planning to steal from them. You may not only be showcasing your expensive items on social media—you may also be becoming a victim.

Examples of Celebrities Robbed of Their Stuff

US rapper PnB Rock, whose real name is Rakim Hasheem Allen, was fatally shot in 2018 during an apparent robbery at a Los Angeles restaurant. He was with his girlfriend when a gunman reportedly demanded jewelry before opening fire inside the Waffle House. Police suggest an Instagram post may have led to the shooting because people knew where he would be eating. After PnB Rock's death, Ice-T said that some rappers skip jewelry because L.A. is "dangerous." LA is not the only dangerous city when it comes to personal robberies and carjackings—all major towns have news stories about these crimes.

As another example, Kim Kardashian had millions of dollars' worth of jewelry stolen during her trip to Paris Fashion Week, which she documented on Instagram.

Example of Non-Celebrities Robbed of Their Expensive Items

In Charlotte, North Carolina, a 17-year-old was shot and killed during a dispute over a pair of sneakers. Apparently, $2,000+ Jordan sneakers are popular among teenagers and young adults.

A 14-year-old child in DC was just walking to the door of his middle school when another teen came up to him and stole his iPhone and $1,200 Black Moose Knuckles coat.

An Atlanta, Georgia, woman was carjacked at gunpoint as thieves stole her Range Rover.

Your Pursuit of Fame on Social Media Could Get You in Trouble

Some people are too self-absorbed in their pursuit of being popular. These people post their lives on social media, showing off their luxury items, fancy homes, expensive cars, and money. Others give details about their location and when they are away from home. Some of these postings make you an easy target. We covered social media in Chapter 5, so remember to avoid showing thieves what you have and where they can steal it.

Key Takeaways

In this chapter, I pointed out that you must be careful with expensive items because thieves are watching. I gave examples not to scare you but to remind you that living a luxurious lifestyle can bring risks.

Your Next Steps

If you decide to buy expensive things, think carefully about the social media posts you share.

Conclusion

"Success is not how high you have climbed, but how you make a positive difference to the world" — Roy T. Bennett

In Part 1, we covered how to recognize your talents, showcase them, identify and enjoy your passions, and enable parents to build confidence and self-esteem in their children. We highlighted some of the benefits and risks of social media. Steve Jobs once said, "The only way to do great work is to love what you do. If you have not found it yet, keep looking."

In Part 2, we covered how to assess your strengths and weaknesses, how to identify your mentors, asked you to decide how you want feedback, focused on learning from your mistakes, and asked you to document your skills development plan. Confucius once said, "Success depends upon previous preparation, and without such preparation, there is sure to be failure." Charlie Batch added to that point, saying, "Proper preparation prevents poor performance."

In Part 3, we covered how to develop a purpose-driven lifestyle and a lifestyle model to achieve balance in life. We also asked you to establish goals, and we helped you understand the importance of close friends. We helped you understand the economic cycle you live in that dictates how you make money and made clear the need to learn new skills continuously. Andrew Carnegie said, "If you want to be happy, set a goal that commands your thoughts, liberates your energy, and inspires your hopes."

In Part 4, we covered how to change your relationship with money, reviewed the fundamentals of money and investing, showed how to get money to work hard for you while you sleep, demonstrated how to break the cycle of poverty, explained how to build financial literacy, and explained how to build a great credit score and save for retirement. We also made an argument for why young adults should start businesses early in life. Many wealthy people live by the idea, "Stop working hard for your money and make money work hard for you."

In Part 5, we explained what a legacy is and how to live yours daily. We asked you to decide how you would help others over your lifetime and gave examples of how you would share your legacy with family and friends. Remember, Leo Buscaglia said, "Your talent is God's gift to you. What you do with it is your gift back to God."

In Part 6, we explained the reality that most of what you see on TV is fake and designed to make money for the studios. Some social media stars lie about traveling in private planes and traveling the world, and many of the products and gadgets they promote are given to them by companies to review and push on unsuspecting fans. The point is to get you to spend money to make everyone else wealthy. Therefore, you should not pursue a lifestyle based on these false notions of life. We gave examples of wealthy people who do not waste money on extravagant material items. We wrapped up Part 6 by highlighting that wearing fancy clothes, jewelry, and flashing smartphones can put your life in danger in most places. Criminals are on the lookout for Jordan sneakers, iPhones, and expensive cars and will kill to take your possessions. Some celebrities were killed in public view because their expensive items were visible. Because of this, most people in Hollywood understand that you have to hide your jewelry when you are out and about.

Call to Action

"Winners are losers who got up
and gave it one more try"

Dennis
DeYoung

At the end of each chapter, we asked you to take action and do something to ensure your success with what you learned. Let us recap all the actions below for your use with mentors, parents, and friends. We hope you enjoyed reading this book, and more importantly, we hope you implement the actions. If you do, you can change the game of how you pursue purpose in life and how you make money. Even if you want to get a college degree, pursue a traditional career, and make lots of money, you can still implement many of these actions to bring more joy to your life.

In Part 1, Recognizing Your Talents and Passion, we asked you to take these actions.

1. Think about and capture your talents and passions on the form at the end of this book.

2. Engage a parent, teacher, or mentor to help you recognize your talents and passions.

3. Write down how you can practice or showcase these talents and passions.

4. You should have used your highlighter during the passion chapter to notate examples you want to think more about.

5. Get your mentor or parent to help you complete the Skills to Passion Assessment Model. It may seem complicated, but it works. Start with your talents from your Chapter 1 list, identify passions from that list, identify skills that enable those passions, identify job titles that require those skills, and then identify companies that offer those jobs.

6. You may need to pull in your school guidance counselor to help with that previous one. Another great resource is SCORE, the Service Corps of Retired Executives.

7. The action for parents is to understand that you were never given a "how to" book on being a parent. That means you must admit when you make mistakes and acknowledge you do not know everything about developing a child. It also means you must seek out parents who do a better job or have better outcomes. There is nothing wrong with getting expert advice, and your child will be better for it. Put aside your pride and realize the world is changing fast.

8. The action for teenagers is to understand and acknowledge that parents are doing the best they can and want the best outcome for you. Teenagers must be more open to longer, deeper, and more engaging conversations.

9. You must think carefully about how you use social media and what you share.

10. Jot down an inventory of what you do and decide what needs to change on social media.

11. Write down what you should continue to do and what you will stop doing on social media.

12. As parents, you must learn what social media is and how your children use each platform. That means digging deeper and learning how to set security parameters. You must ensure there

are no older adults in your child's friends list that you do not know. It would help if you put a reminder on your calendar to engage with your child about their social media activity and how it makes them feel.

In Part 2, Preparation Enables Success, we asked you to take these actions.

13. Meet with your mentor or parent and complete the Skills to Passion Assessment Model as illustrated in Figure 2. Transfer skills in the right two boxes to your personal development plan so you can improve those skills.

14. Meet with your business mentor and complete the Skills to Jobs Mapping Model as illustrated in Figure 3. This exercise will show how selecting your dream job is tied to your preferred skills that align with your passion.

15. Discuss your team of mentors with your parents or best friend, then select your mentors. Complete the Success Team Mentor List form at the end of this book.

16. Share the role definition with each mentor and get their buy-in and agreement to fulfill that role.

17. Think through and decide how you want your feedback from your mentors.

18. Set up quarterly feedback sessions with each mentor so you do not miss any ideas.

19. Nothing good will happen sitting on the couch. If you fail at first, get up quickly and try again, learning from your mistakes. Your action is not to be afraid to do something.

20. Teenagers, parents, and mentors must work together to develop a personal development plan. Remember, perfection is a flaw, so do not waste time trying to perfect it. The most important thing is the skills you find necessary and getting started quickly.

21. Add a date to your calendar so you can review and inspect your personal development progress and update your status for each activity.

In Part 3, Live A Purpose-Driven Life, we asked you to take these actions.

22. Develop your life-balance model based on the four cornerstones discussed. Your time allocations may change depending on your priorities for spending time with family or friends. Ultimately, your passion should drive your purpose and how you make your income.

23. Complete the Behavior Change Planning Model indicated in Figure 5.

24. Write down your goals. To do that, meet with your mentors, parents, and friends to discuss your future vision of life and ask for their input on how you should get there. After a robust and challenging discussion, write down your three-year goals.

25. Think carefully about your friend list and decide who your close or intimate friends are. Narrow your list down to the top five you desire to be your lifelong advisors. Call them and discuss what you need from them and confirm they want to fulfill that role. Next, run the list by your parents because they may know things about your friends that you do not know.

26. Study and research how money is made in the 21st century. Do not be afraid to discuss this with your parents, using the idea of challenging old norms and methods. Once you meet with your mentor and know how money can be made, adjust your talents, passion, and skills assessment before implementing your learning development plan.

In Part 4, Change Your Relationship with Money, we asked you to take these actions.

27. Request a copy of your credit report.

28. We covered SMART goals in Chapter 12, so do not forget to set financial goals and update your goals tracking sheet to include your new financial goals.

29. Learn more about compound interest.

30. Invest in your 401K at work and use a ROTH IRA if you jump from job to job. You do not just want to invest—you want to max out your contributions so your money can work its magic.

31. Complete and review your budget for ways to find $100 per month to invest.

32. Track your spending for 30 days to see where your money is going and how you can keep more of it.

33. If applicable, schedule a meeting with grandparents and explain how they can help get your child, their grandchild, out of poverty.

34. Speak with someone who understands accounting and the income limits for a child's earned income.

35. Find a family member with a business and ask them to use your child in their marketing efforts for a fee. They usually pay good money to others, so do not hesitate to ask for more.

36. Meet with your parents and mentors and decide if you should start a business early in life. If you choose to start a business, follow all the steps outlined in Chapter 18.

In Part 5, Build and Live Your Legacy, we asked you to take these actions.

37. Develop a personal mission statement that captures your values, principles, goals, and aspirations. This concise statement can serve as a guide, helping you stay focused on your legacy-

building efforts. Your mentors, parents, and friends can help you with this task.

38. Think about living authentically, true to your values and beliefs. This exercise includes thinking about what personality you desire. Consider the life you want 10 years from now.

39. Decide how you will help others. You can start a blog, podcast, or nonprofit or write a book about how you solved a problem. Others are looking for solutions to the same issues. People of all ages can volunteer at a local charity.

40. Reflect on how helping others will help you in return. Write down the benefits of your experience so you can share them with others to inspire them.

41. Complete the legacy checklist in Figure 10 at the end of the book.

42. Decide which of the 13 legacy ideas you will implement. Do not forget to save your work to your Google Drive folder named for your legacy.

43. Consider all the advice examples and decide if you need to change your prior decisions, goals, and plans.

44. Ask your parents, grandparents, aunts, and uncles to do this exercise so they can share their experiences and recommendations with you. Make changes as necessary.

45. Read the short book *Who Moved My Cheese?* to understand the concept of "don't sweat the small stuff."

In Part 6, Don't Believe Everything You See on TV, we asked you to take these actions.

46. Use the chapters of this book to develop your own lifestyle based on your talents, passions, and skills. Be unique and enjoy each moment of life as a unique path just for you.

47. Reflect back on Part 4, Changing Your Relationship with Money, and develop a philosophy where you can build wealth instead of living wealthy. It would help if you could discuss this with your parents, friends, and mentors for input.

48. If you decide to buy expensive items, think carefully about your social media posts.

49. Evaluate your lifestyle to see if you are patterning your behavior based on the example you see on social media or TV. Then, decide if you must change your choices, behavior, and lifestyle.

Take Action Now!

The last thing for you to do is to do something. Schedule your meetings with your parents, mentors, friends, and other advisors so you can get busy.

Write down how you will implement the book's chapter ideas and allow plenty of time to complete your actions without feeling rushed. You should use the action item checklist in Figure 12 to ensure you are progressing well over the next two years.

Download the templates so you can fill them out and capture your decisions. All of the attachments are available on our website at dare2succeed.org.

If you need more help learning how to implement the recommendations, visit dare2succeed.org to learn more about our online video training. We have detailed training modules that teach you how to implement what you learned in each chapter of this book.

This learning collection is called the "Dare to Succeed Learning Lab." We also provide e-books and other resources to help you understand and implement your actions.

DARE2SUCCEED

PASSION • PURPOSE

We understand that some of these solutions may differ from what society suggests, so we are here to help you. If you want one-on-one coaching, contact us at advisor@tips4living.org for a free 30-minute consultation. We can help you understand how to implement each idea. Because we created all the models in this book, we can help you understand how to use them and how to arrive at the best possible decision. You can be assigned a certified life coach, who will guide you with hands-on support.

Our website, tips4living.org, has other great resources, a blog section, and other videos dealing with nutrition, fitness, business, finance, technology, and lifestyle changes. You may sign up to receive tips by email.

You may also find our YouTube channel @tips4living, a great place to find videos on the same topics above.

Acknowledgments

I want to acknowledge the support of my early content readers, proofreaders, and those who gave input to ensure this book has value for teenagers and their parents.

I want to publicly show appreciation to my wife for her patience and support as I locked myself away to write this book.

About the Author

Richard A. Sherrod Sr. is a book author dedicated to reducing the mental health epidemic in the world among young adults. His focus is helping young adults find their passions and purpose in life, reduce their despair, and help them make money based on their passions. He is the founder and CEO of the Sherrod Foundation Inc., a 501(c)(3) nonprofit charity dedicated to helping teenagers, young adults, and their parents get the business and finance skills needed to succeed. With over 40 years of corporate experience, he completed many volunteer charity projects to support children and their parents. Richard worked in the technology industry as a vice president, strategy manager, finance manager, customer satisfaction manager, and engineer. He is a certified trainer, certified master life coach, expert facilitator, certified Lean Six Sigma Green belt, and process expert.

Richard and his wife Dolores started a coaching business, Tips4Living LLC, to help others solve common problems preventing them from achieving success. He helps others learn how to build wealth or live a lifestyle based on their passions. He has been married for over 44 years and knows the challenges of being a parent, and that is why he started a podcast called *Building a Great Marriage* to help people improve their relationships. As a man of faith, he loves teaching Christian living in the 21st century.

Richard has completed several projects, and several more are coming in the next four years, so check out his work at sherrodfamily.com.

Attachments

Figure 1 – Living by Passion Success Model

Figure 2 – Passion to Skills Assessment Model

Figure 3 – Skills to Jobs Mapping Model

Figure 4 – Success Team Mentor List Form

Figure 5 – Personal Development Plan Form

Figure 6 – Behavior Change Planning Model

Figure 7 – Goals Tracking Form

Figure 8 – Do's and Don'ts of Managing Good Credit

Figure 9 – New Ways to Market Your Business

Figure 10 – Legacy Checklist

Figure 11 – Memory Sheet Sample

Figure 12   Action Item Checklist

Because you purchased this book, you may download any attachments, models, forms, samples, or checklists from our website, dare2succeed.org. Some electronic models and forms have blank sheets to fill in your information as you work with mentors, friends, and parents.

Join our Facebook group, Dare2Succeed, and share your story as you work through finding your passions and living a purpose-driven lifestyle.

Figure 1

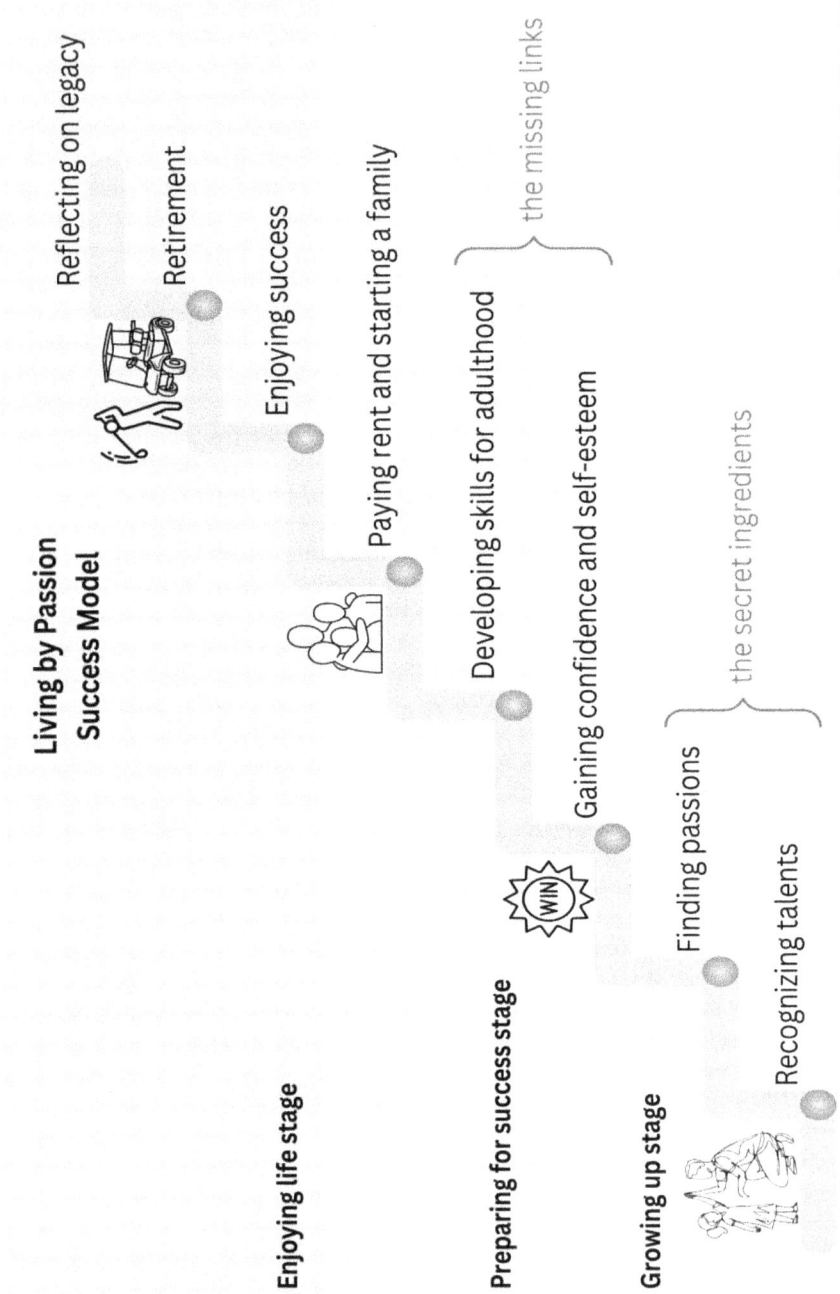

Living by Passion Success Model

Enjoying life stage
- Reflecting on legacy
- Retirement
- Enjoying success

Preparing for success stage
- Paying rent and starting a family — *the missing links*
- Developing skills for adulthood
- Gaining confidence and self-esteem

Growing up stage
- Finding passions — *the secret ingredients*
- Recognizing talents

Figure 2

**Passion to Skills
Assessment Model**

What skills do you like using and are good at?	What skills do you like using but are not good at?
Enter your response	Enter your response
Practice and sell these skills.	Add these skills to your improvement plan.
What skills do you dislike using but are good at?	**What skills do you dislike using and are not good at?**
Enter your response	Enter your response
Tolerate these skills because they are necessary.	Some skills are needed, so add them to your improvement plan. Others can be ignored.

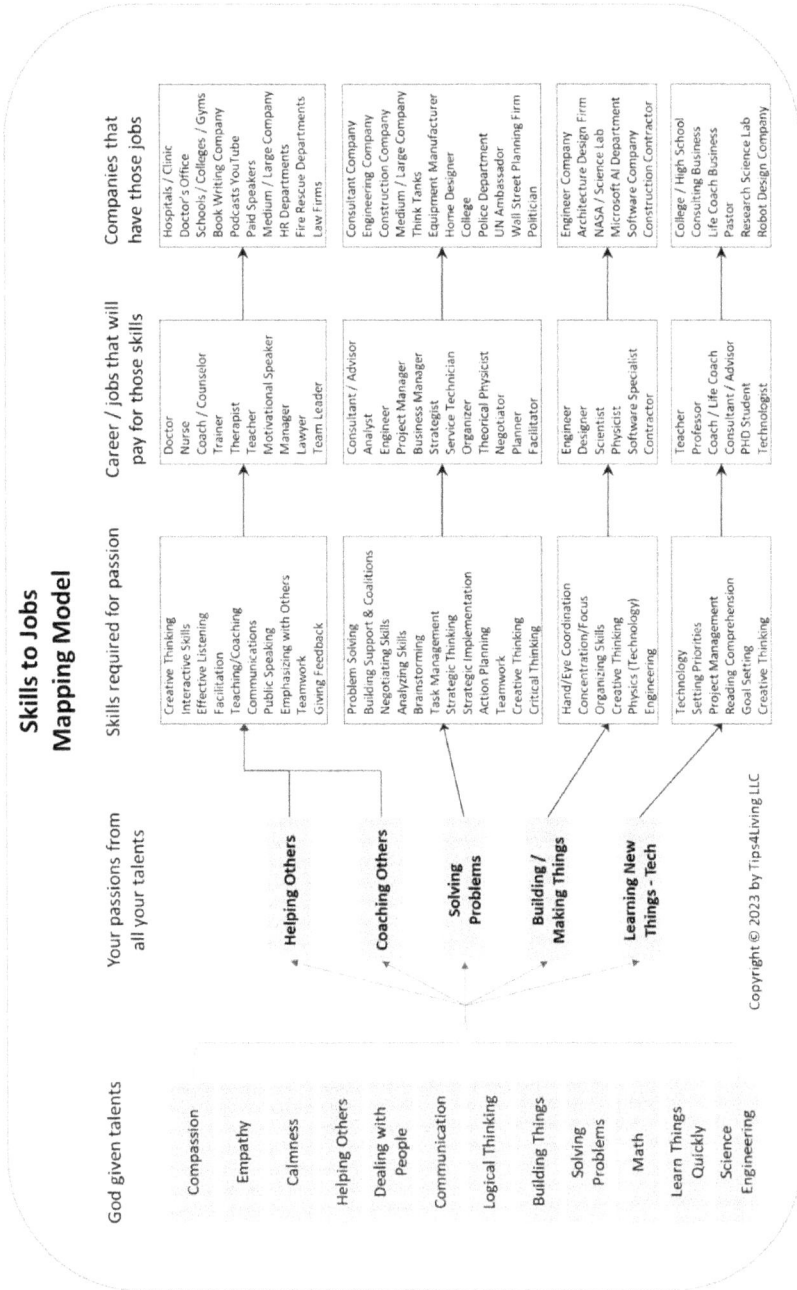

Figure 3

Skills to Jobs Mapping Model

God given talents

- Compassion
- Empathy
- Calmness
- Helping Others
- Dealing with People
- Communication
- Logical Thinking
- Building Things
- Solving Problems
- Math
- Learn Things Quickly
- Science
- Engineering

Your passions from all your talents

- Helping Others
- Coaching Others
- Solving Problems
- Building / Making Things
- Learning New Things - Tech

Skills required for passion

- Creative Thinking
- Interactive Skills
- Effective Listening
- Facilitation
- Teaching/Coaching
- Communications
- Public Speaking
- Emphasizing with Others
- Teamwork
- Giving Feedback

- Problem Solving
- Building Support & Coalitions
- Negotiating Skills
- Analyzing Skills
- Brainstorming
- Task Management
- Strategic Implementation
- Action Planning
- Teamwork
- Creative Thinking
- Critical Thinking

- Hand/Eye Coordination
- Concentration/Focus
- Organizing Skills
- Creative Thinking
- Physics (Technology)
- Engineering

- Technology
- Setting Priorities
- Project Management
- Reading Comprehension
- Goal Setting
- Creative Thinking

Career / jobs that will pay for those skills

- Doctor
- Nurse
- Coach / Counselor
- Trainer
- Therapist
- Teacher
- Motivational Speaker
- Manager
- Lawyer
- Team Leader

- Consultant / Advisor
- Analyst
- Engineer
- Project Manager
- Business Manager
- Strategist
- Service Technician
- Organizer
- Theorical Physicist
- Negotiator
- Planner
- Facilitator

- Engineer
- Designer
- Scientist
- Physicist
- Software Specialist
- Contractor

- Teacher
- Professor
- Coach / Life Coach
- Consultant / Advisor
- PhD Student
- Technologist

Companies that have those jobs

- Hospitals / Clinic
- Doctor's Office
- Schools / Colleges / Gyms
- Book Writing Company
- Podcasts YouTube
- Paid Speakers
- Medium / Large Company
- HR Departments
- Fire Rescue Departments
- Law Firms

- Consultant Company
- Engineering Company
- Construction Company
- Medium / Large Company
- Think Tanks
- Equipment Manufacturer
- Home Designer
- College
- Police Department
- UN Ambassador
- Wall Street Planning Firm
- Politician

- Engineer Company
- Architecture Design Firm
- NASA / Science Lab
- Microsoft AI Department
- Software Company
- Construction Contractor

- College / High School
- Consulting Business
- Life Coach Business
- Pastor
- Research Science Lab
- Robot Design Company

Figure 4

Success Team Mentor List

Role	Responsibilities	Mentor Name	Mentor Experience	Feedback Method
Motivational & Spiritual Mentor	This person will help you with finding out who you are. As you develop your values, style, personality, principles and behavior traits, this person will serve as your mirror. They will confirm your view of self is what other people see and recommend action when the two don't align. This person will help you with your talents, passions and enjoyment of life. This person must be upbeat, optimistic and one who does good for the sake of good.			
Business & Finance Mentor	This person will help you with managing money. They will ensure you have a FICA credit score above 700 and help you avoid common mistakes for managing debt and credit cards. They will ensure you understand 'compound interest' and how this is the secret to building wealth while working. If you have a desire to start you own business, they will be your source of advice and coaching. Think of business owners, company managers, CPA's or finance managers. Anyone with an MBA will meet the requirements.			
Training & Development Mentor	This person will help you with your skills, training and talent development. They will advise you on AP classes to take in high school and prepare you for college. They will also help you align your skills with a career so you can live a life of joy, while being paid for what you love. Think of teachers, trainers and college development personnel for this role. Most people have teachers in their family, so this person shouldn't be hard to find.			
Health & Wellness Mentor	This person should have expertise in healthy eating, fitness and mental health wellness. Taking care of your body, mind and soul is critical to living a life of purpose and passion. Stress, anxiety and depression sometimes come as a result of bad health, excess weight or lack of peace. Think of nurses, doctors, therapists, dietitians, and personal gym trainers for this role.			
Goals & Project Management Mentor	This person should have training or experience with setting short and long-term goals. They will get deep into conversations about your goals and help you plan a course of action to achieve them. They will make sure you have a tracking method for each goal or mini-goal and follow up with you on getting them done. They will help you balance all the stuff you have to do and help organize and prioritize them. Think of program/project managers at work or people with skills in Microsoft Office software for tracking tasks.			

Figure 5

Personal Development Plan

What – Skill	Why – reason for doing it	How – Activity To Improve	When – Due Date	Where – Method	Status
Public Speaking Skill	Communicate with confidence	Complete Toastmasters	June 2024	Local Church	Pending
Effective Listening Skill	To understand another person's needs	Complete an online class	July 2024	LinkedIn online classes	Pending
Coaching others	Provide ideas and support to others	Complete Life Coaching Certification	August 2024	Online website	Pending
Negotiating Skill	To be able to agree on difficult issues	Complete an online class	September 2024	LinkedIn online classes	Pending
Facilitation Skill	Facilitate others to agreement on issues	Complete an online class	October 2024	LinkedIn online classes	Pending
Presentation Software	Present ideas to others in meetings	Complete a Microsoft PowerPoint class	November 2024	Microsoft online learning	Pending
Finance Skills	Manage money successfully	Complete multiple classes on finance	December 2024	Nonprofit Workshops	Pending
Writing Skills	Be able to write a book or podcast	Complete classes on writing	March 2025	Book writers' club online	Pending
Team Player Skills	Work as a team member to achieve goals	Complete interactive skills class online	July 2025	LinkedIn online classes	Pending
Computer Skills	Use a computer well to achieve tasks	Complete a computer user class	August 2025	Nonprofit Workshops	Pending

Figure 6

Behavior Change Planning Model

What behaviors are helpful for your future that you are doing and should continue doing?

Enter your response

These behaviors are good and need to continue

What behaviors are not helpful for your future that you are doing now but must stop doing?

Enter your response

These behaviors are bad. I keep doing them but must stop

What behaviors are helpful for your future that you are not currently doing but should start doing?

Enter your response

These behaviors are good, but I am not doing them now

What behavior is not helpful for your future that you are not doing now and must ensure you never do?

Enter your response

These behaviors are bad, and I don't ever want to do them

Figure 7

My Goals

	Description of goal	Why do I want this goal and what is the desired outcome?	When will I achieve it?	What happens if this goal is not met?	How will I measure this goal?	What are my weekly milestones of achievement?	Status?
Main Goal #1 =							
mini goal #1 =							
mini goal #2 =							
mini goal #3 =							
Main Goal #2 =							
mini goal #1 =							
mini goal #2 =							
mini goal #3 =							
Main Goal #3 =							
mini goal #1 =							
mini goal #2 =							
mini goal #3 =							

Figure 8

Do's & Don'ts of Managing Great Credit

Do

☐ Pay your bills on time

☐ Pay down debt

☐ Keep some accounts open even after paid

☐ Take responsibility for your financial health

☐ Keep you utilization rates at 10% or less

☐ Seek professional help when you don't know what to do

☐ Monitor your credit regularly

Don't

☐ Pay for a service you can perform yourself

☐ Use a credit settlement company

☐ Spend more than you earn, pay with cash

☐ Allow negative credit to stand in the way of your dreams

☐ Stay in the "debt trap"

☐ Don't open a lot of credit card accounts, especially from pre-approved mailers

Figure 9

New Ways To Market Your Business

Get social media marketing training from YouTube

Set up free social media accounts

Pay a Fiveer freelancer to create a logo and brand kit

Pay a Fiveer freelancer to create a launch video for your business

Create a free 'lead magnet' to offer website visitors to get their email

Build a large email list to use with email marketing

Set up an expo table at a women's conference

Use a nonprofit or foundation to get a grant to pay for your marketing expenses

Figure 10

Legacy Checklist

Action	Investment 1=zero 2=low 3=moderate	Status	Comments
Developing Your Legacy			
Self-Reflection and Identity			
Identify your values, principles and beliefs	1		use 'Skills to Passion Assessment Model'
Identify your natural talents given by God	2		use 'Skills to Passion Assessment Model'
Identify your passions	1		use 'Skills to Passion Assessment Model'
Identify the personality you want to have	1		
Develop a personal mission statement for your life's journey.	1		
Goal Setting			
Define personal and professional goals.	1		use goal tracking form
Break down goals into mini goals	1		use goal tracking form
Develop your milestones to check on progress	1		use goal tracking form
Personal Growth			
Identify skills development opportunities for your PDP.	2		use personal development plan form
Develop a schedule to meet with mentors	1		
Budget for continuous learning and skill development.	2		classes can be done online for free
Develop a routine for requesting personal feedback	1		
Cultivate a growth mindset.	1		
Relationship Building			
Foster positive and meaningful connections with family, friends, neighbors and mentors.	1		
Develop a schedule for contacting loved ones	1		
Learn negotiating skills	1		classes can be done online for free
Learn problem solving skills	1		classes can be done online for free
Health and Well-being			
Develop a physical fitness plan	3		gym membership, exercise equipment
Develop a mental health improvement plan	2		doctor visits, vacation plans, hobbies
Develop a plan for spiritual health improvement	1		Church, yoga, meditation
Develop methods for taking time outs or breaks from things	1		
Develop and maintain healthy eating habits.	2		vegetarian or vegan eating styles
Helping Others and Giving Back			
Volunteer at organizations that align with your values.	1		
Donate to charitable nonprofits.	3		
Write a book on an expertise you developed after 20 years	2		self-publishing is easier to get started
Start a blog or podcast to share your knowledge	2		
Mentor a teenager or young adult	1		

Figure 11

Memory Sheet

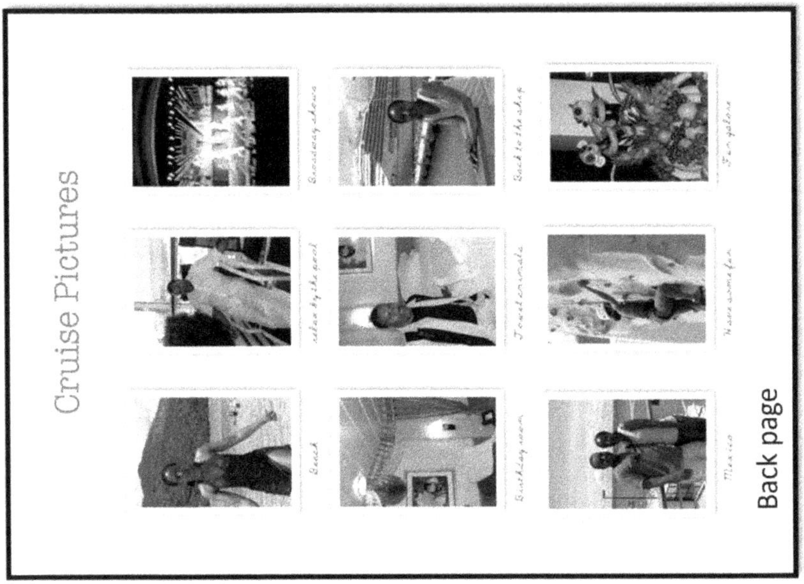
Cruise Pictures
Back page

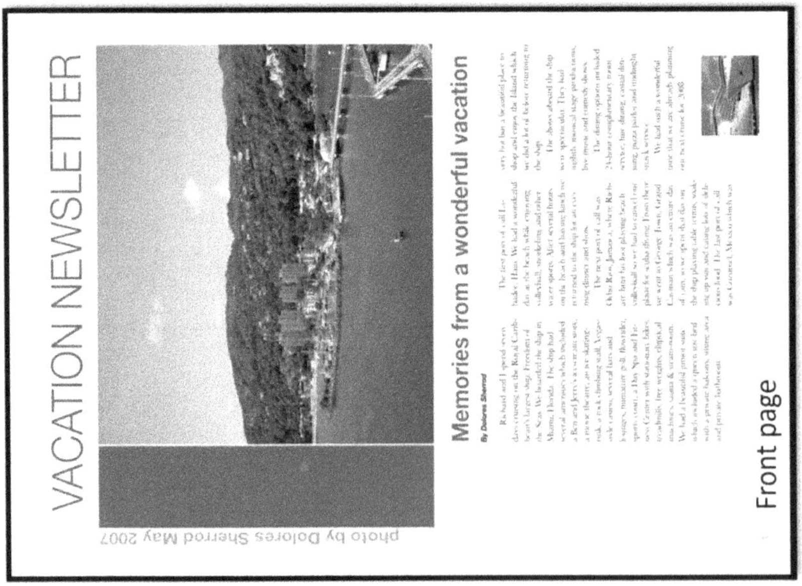
VACATION NEWSLETTER
photo by Dolores Sherrod May 2007
Memories from a wonderful vacation
By Dolores Sherrod
Front page

Figure 12

Dare To Succeed Action Item Checklist

Action	Status
Part 2 - Preparation Enables Success	
Meet with your mentor or parent and complete the Skills to Passion Assessment Model as illustrated in Figure 2. Transfer skills in the right two boxes to your personal development plan so you can improve those skills.	
Meet with your business mentor and complete the Skills to Jobs Mapping Model as illustrated in Figure 3. This exercise will show how selecting your dream job is tied to your preferred skills that align with your passion.	
Discuss your team of mentors with your parents or best friend, then select your mentors. Complete the Success Team Mentor List form at the end of this book.	
Share the role definition with each mentor and get their buy-in and agreement to fulfill that role.	
Think through and decide how you want your feedback from your mentors.	
Set up quarterly feedback sessions with each mentor so you do not miss any ideas.	
Nothing good will happen sitting on the couch. If you fail at first, get up quickly and try again, learning from your mistakes. Your action is not to be afraid to do something.	
Teenagers, parents, and mentors must work together to develop a personal development plan. Remember, perfection is a flaw, so do not waste time trying to perfect it. The most important thing is the skills you find necessary and getting started quickly.	
Add a date to your calendar so you can review and inspect your personal development progress and update your status for each activity.	

References

"Benefits of Mentoring for Young People." n.d. *Youth.gov*. Accessed October 19, 2023. https://youth.gov/youth-topics/mentoring/benefits-mentoring-young-people.

Carroll, Joseph. "Americans Satisfied with Number of Friends, Closeness of Friendships." 2004. *Gallup.com*. March 5, 2004. https://news.gallup.com/poll/10891/americans-satisfied-number-friends-closeness-friendships.aspx.

CliftonStrengths. n.d. Accessed October 18, 2023. https://www.gallup.com/cliftonstrengths/en/254033/strengthsfinder.aspx.

Degges-White, Suzanne. 2019. "How Many Friends Do You Really Need in Adulthood?" *Psychology Today*. August 9, 2019. https://www.psychologytoday.com/us/blog/lifetime-connections/201908/how-many-friends-do-you-really-need-in-adulthood.

Fisher, Sean. 2024. "Warren Buffet: 12 Things Poor People Squander Money On." *Yahoo Finance*. April 22, 2024. https://finance.yahoo.com/news/warren-buffett-12-things-poor-143028989.html.

"Manorialism Summary." n.d. *Britannica*. Accessed May 2, 2020. https://www.britannica.com/summary/manorialism.

Sherrod – Dare to Succeed

Pino, Ivana. 2022. "The Average Net Worth of Baby Boomers, Who Are Expected to Pass on $53 Trillion When They Die." *Fortune*. December 30, 2022. https://fortune.com/recommends/investing/baby-boomers-average-net-worth/.

"Official Myers-Briggs Test and Personality Assessment." n.d. *MBTIonline*. Accessed October 18, 2023. https://www.mbtionline.com/.

SCORE. n.d. Accessed October 19, 2023. https://www.score.org/.

242

www.ingramcontent.com/pod-product-compliance
Lightning Source LLC
Chambersburg PA
CBHW071214090426
42736CB00014B/2811